WHAT THE CRITICS SAY:

A very worthwhile addition to any travel libr

Armed with these guides, you may never a

Easily carried ... neatly organized ... wond........ ...... to my travel library. The authors wax as enthusiastically as I do about the almost too-quaint-to-believe Country Inns. —**San Francisco Chronicle**

One can only welcome such guide books and wish them long, happy, and healthy lives in print. —**Wichita Kansas Eagle**

This series of pocket-sized paperbacks will guide travelers to hundreds of little known and out of the way inns, lodges, and historic hotels.... a thorough menu. —**(House Beautiful's) Colonial Homes**

Charming, extremely informative, clear and easy to read; excellent travelling companions. —**Books-Across-The-Sea** *(The English Speaking Union)*

...a fine selection of inviting places to stay... provide excellent guidance.... —**Blair & Ketchum's Country Journal**

Obviously designed for our kind of travel.... [the authors] have our kind of taste. —**Daily Oklahoman**

The first guidebook was so successful that they have now taken on the whole nation.... Inns are chosen for charm, architectural style, location, furnishings and history. —**Portland Oregonian**

Many quaint and comfy country inns throughout the United States... The authors have a grasp of history and legend. —**Dallas (Tx.) News**

Very fine travel guides. —**Santa Ana (Calif.) Register**

A wonderful source for planning trips. —**Northampton (Mass.) Gazette**

...pocketsize books full of facts.... attractively made and illustrated. —**New York Times Book Review**

Hundreds of lovely country inns reflecting the charm and hospitality of various areas throughout the U.S. —**Youngstown (Ohio) Vindicator**

Some genius must have measured the average American dashboard, because the Compleat Traveler's Companions fit right between the tissues and bananas on our last trip.... These are good-looking books with good-looking photographs.... very useful.

—**East Hampton (N.Y.) Star**

ALSO AVAILABLE IN THE COMPLEAT TRAVELER SERIES

- ☐ *Ferguson's* Europe by Eurail: *How to Tour Europe by Train*

- ☐ *Ferguson's* Britain by BritRail: *How to Tour Britain by Train*

- ☐ *Fistell's* America by Train: *How to Tour America by Rail*

- ☐ Bed & Breakfast America: *Great American Guest House Book*

- ☐ National & State Parks: *Lodges, Cabins, & Resorts*

- ☐ MacNeice: *National Sites, Monuments, and Battlefields*

- ☐ **Country Inns** & Historic Hotels of Great Britain

- ☐ **Country Inns** & Historic Hotels of Canada

- ☐ **Country Inns** & Historic Hotels of Ireland

- ☐ **Country** New England **Inns**

- ☐ **Country Inns** & Historic Hotels of the Middle Atlantic States

- ☐ **Country Inns** & Historic Hotels of the South

- ☐ **Country Inns** & Historic Hotels of the Midwest & Rocky Mts.

- ☐ **Country Inns** & Historic Hotels of California & the Northwest

- ☐ Guide to Country New England

- ☐ Guide to California & Pacific N.W.

- ☐ Guide to Texas and the Southwest

- ☐ *Scheer's* Guide to Virginia

- ☐ *Scheer's* Guide to North Carolina

- ☐ *Scheer's* Guide to Tennessee

- ☐ *Scheer's* Guide to Florida

If your local bookseller, gift shop, or country inn does not stock a particular title, ask them to order directly from Burt Franklin & Co., Inc., 235 East 44th Street, New York, 10017, U.S.A. Telephone orders are accepted from recognized retailers and credit-card holders. In the U.S.A., call, toll-free, 1-800-223-0766 during regular business hours. (In New York State, call 212-687-5250.)

Midwest & Rockies

COUNTRY INNS
Lodges & Historic Hotels

Anthony Hitchcock & Jean Lindgren

BURT FRANKLIN & COMPANY, INC.

Published by
BURT FRANKLIN & COMPANY
235 East Forty-fourth Street
New York, New York 10017

Copyright © 1979, 1980, 1981, 1982, 1983,
1984, 1985, 1986, and 1987 by Burt Franklin & Co., Inc.

Library of Congress Cataloging in Publication Data

Hitchcock, Anthony
Country inns, lodges, and historic hotels of the
Midwest and Rocky Mountain States
(The Compleat traveler's companion)
Includes index.
1. Hotels, taverns, etc.—Middle West—Directories.
2. Hotels, taverns, etc.—Rocky Mountains region—Directories.
I. Lindgren, Jean, joint author.
II. Title.   III. Series: Compleat traveler's companion.
TX907 .H5392   1987   647'.947701
ISBN 0-89102-356-9 (pbk.)

Cover illustration courtesy of
The Whitmore
Nephi, Utah

Manufactured in the United States of America
1 3 4 2

THE GREAT LAKES REGION

THE CENTRAL STATES

THE ROCKIES

Introduction

In this new edition, we have quoted the most recent room rates in a combined rate chart and index at the end of the book. Readers should note that the listed rates are *subject to change*. While the quoted rates are for double occupancy in most cases, single travelers as well as larger groups should inquire about special rates. We list daily room rates as based on the American Plan (AP, all three meals included), Modified American Plan (MAP, breakfast and dinner included), Bed and Breakfast (BB, either full or Continental breakfast included), or European Plan (EP, no meals). In many cases a tax and a service charge will be added. Be sure to ask. Children and pets present special problems for many inns. If either is *not* welcome at an inn it is noted in the description. These regulations also often change, and it is imperative that families traveling with either inquire in advance. Though many inns state they are open all year, we find that many close during slow periods. Call first to confirm your room reservations.

The inns described in this book were chosen for their inherent charm, based partially on their architectural style, location, furnishings, and history. We have made every effort to provide information as carefully and accurately as possible, but we remind readers that all listed rates and schedules are subject to change. Further, we have neither solicited nor accepted any fees or gratuities for being included in this book or any of the other books in this series. We have tried to be responsive to reader suggestions arising out of earlier editions of this book. Should readers wish to offer suggestions for future editions, we welcome their correspondence. Please write to us in care of our publishers: Burt Franklin and Company, 235 East Forty-fourth Street, New York, NY 10017. JEAN LINDGREN
ANTHONY HITCHCOCK

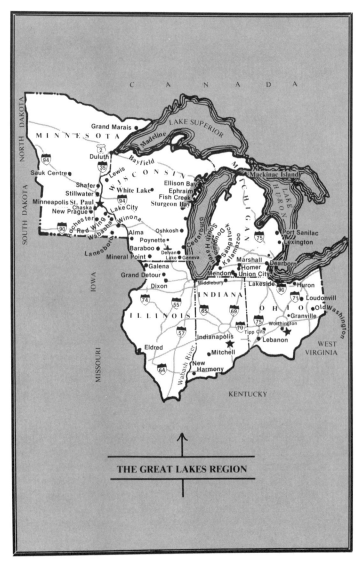

THE GREAT LAKES REGION

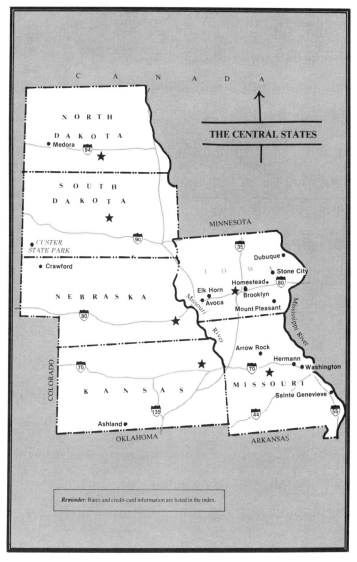

THE CENTRAL STATES

C A N A D A

NORTH
DAKOTA
● Medora ⟨94⟩ ★

SOUTH
DAKOTA ★

● CUSTER
STATE PARK

MINNESOTA

● Crawford

NEBRASKA ⟨90⟩

⟨35⟩

I O W A

Dubuque ●
Stone City ●

Elk Horn ● Homestead ● ⟨80⟩
Avoca ● ★ Brooklyn
Mount Pleasant ●

Missouri River

Mississippi River

⟨80⟩ ★

COLORADO ⟨70⟩

★

Arrow Rock ●
Hermann ●
⟨70⟩ ● Washington
★

K A N S A S
⟨135⟩

MISSOURI
Sainte Genevieve ●

Ashland ●
⟨44⟩ ⟨55⟩

OKLAHOMA

ARKANSAS

Reminder: Rates and credit-card information are listed in the index.

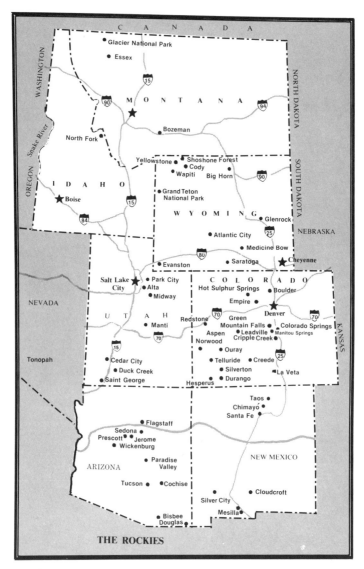

THE ROCKIES

The Great Lakes

Illinois

Dixon, Illinois

RIVERVIEW GUEST HOUSE

507 E. Everett Street, Dixon, IL 61021. 815-288-5974. *Innkeepers:* Ed and Mary Lou Evett. Open all year.

Dixon was the boyhood home of President Reagan. The Rock River flows through the village, and the Riverhead Guest House offers a view of the river and a small park at the water's edge. Mary Lou and Ed have opened their 1890 Victorian home to overnight guests. Gas lamps have been electrified, and bathrooms and the kitchen have been modernized, but time appears to have stood still in the rest of the house. Oak filigree separates the front parlor from the music room, with its Victorian potted palm alongside an upright piano and a Victrola. Breakfast is served in the oak-paneled dining room, with its late period furnishings, or out on the lacy wicker sun porch, home to many hanging plants. Guest rooms have beds with antique quilts and feature views of the river.

Accommodations: 3 rooms with shared baths. *Pets:* Not permitted. *Driving Instructions:* From I-5, take Route 26 (Galena Avenue) to Everett Street. Turn right. The inn is on the left.

HOBSON'S BLUFFDALE

Eldred-Hillview Road, Eldred, Illinois. Mailing address: Route 1, Eldred, IL 62027. 217-983-2854. *Innkeepers:* Bill and Lindy Hobson. Open April to December.

Bill Hobson's great-great-grandfather John Russell bought the land for Hobson's farm from the U.S. Government in 1818. Russell, an author whose poems appeared in *McGuffy's Fifth Reader*, built the Federalist-Georgian farmhouse ten years later from native limestone quarried from the nearby river bluffs. The walls are 2 feet thick and the house has six fireplaces, originally the only source of heat. John Russell, a great admirer of Charles Dickens, corresponded with him for many years. When Dickens was touring America he was a guest at Bluffdale. Great-great-grandmother Russell had very strong anti-slavery convictions. Sometime before the Civil War someone came to the farm bearing a petition to make Illinois a slave state. He handed the petition to Grandmother Russell as she sat before the huge fireplace in her kitchen. She read the words and gazed thoughtfully at the long list of names supporting its tenets, then silently, dropped the petition behind the blazing backlog.

Today, this fireplace, large enough to cook a deer or small steer in, is a dominant feature of the sitting room. When the Hobsons moved into the house (seven generations of Bill's family have now lived there) they found it barely livable by modern standards, and their first efforts were to restore and modernize it. In the process they discovered four walled-up fireplaces upstairs. They added plumbing and a new electrical system, made major improvements to the farm buildings, and built a two-story addition to the house. Finally, as the guest business blossomed at Bluffdale, they built a separate gambrel-roofed "bunkhouse" containing air-conditioned guest rooms and suites that can sleep up to seven.

Lindy and her family start early each day to prepare the three meals served to guests. Working in her large kitchen, she turns out quantities of fine farm cooking. She is particularly proud of her fried chicken, barbecued whole pork, pot roast, and barbecued pork chops. Meals are accompanied by farm-baked breads, sweet rolls, and pies or cakes. In the morning the generous farm breakfast includes sausage and bacon made at Bluffdale. Guests who wish to eat lunch while hiking in the surrounding woods are supplied with picnic lunches.

Bluffdale is a fully operating farm that raises pigs, chickens, sheep, and horses. There is a farrowing house where the baby pigs are born, and the farm usually has pigs at several stages of growth. Guests who wish to understand the entire pig-raising process from beginning to end are welcome to accompany the Hobsons when they take the hogs to market. Most, however, are happy to enjoy the farm activities at Bluffdale and enjoy the surrounding bluffs and hiking trails. The farm has a heated swimming pool and a whirlpool bath. Creeks and the river provide fishing. The Hobsons frequently hold outdoor barbecues and hot dog roasts; square dancing and table tennis are offered in the recreation room. Horseback riding is available over paths that crisscross the 200 acres of the farm, and pony-cart rides are available for the younger children who are guests.

Accommodations: 5 rooms and 3 two-room suites with private bath. *Pets:* Not permitted. *Driving Instructions:* Take Route 108 to Eldred. The farm is 3½ miles north on the Eldred-Hillview Road.

Galena, Illinois

ALDRICH GUEST HOUSE
   900 Third Street, Galena, IL 61036. 815-777-3323. *Innkeepers:* Judy
   Green. Open all year.

In 1867, Senator Robert H. McClellan purchased a large brick house
overlooking the village green where his friend Ulysses S. Grant trained
his troops. The senator's home was the setting for lavish parties honor-
ing the Civil War hero. The innkeeper has retained that earlier elegance
while adding airy curtains, lighter colors, and Oriental carpets and
throw rugs. The double parlor, decorated with period furniture, has
a Steinway grand piano and a fireplace bordered with Delft tiles.

   The guest rooms are furnished with Victorian pieces, including
walnut, oak, brass, and painted-iron beds. The bathrooms have pull-
chain commodes and old-fashioned claw-footed tubs. Breakfasts of
fresh fruits, muffins, breads, and a variety of egg dishes are served
in the dining room. Complimentary wine and soft drinks are offered
in the late afternoon. Judy will gladly help guests plan tours of this
historic town and provide menus from local restaurants.

   Accommodations: 4 rooms, 3 with private bath. *Pets:* Not permitted. *Children:* Under 6 not permitted. *Driving Instructions:* From
Route 20 in Galena, turn north onto Third Street.

BELLE AIRE MANSION

11410 Route 20 West, Galena, IL 61036. 815-777-0893. *Innkeepers:* Evelyn and James Nemecek. Open all year.

Galena is a historic town with many beautiful homes, and Belle Aire Mansion is no exception. This large white Colonial stands on 16 acres of parklike grounds complete with a large old barn and a working windmill. A two-block-long driveway approaches the house between colonnades of 30- to 40-foot pines.

Inside the mansion, beneath the formal, antique-filled parlor and guest rooms, lies the true heart of Belle Aire, a mid-nineteenth-century log cabin. The long-gone denizens of the cabin would certainly be pleased, if a bit confused, to see today the successive additions that have obscured the original hand-hewn timbers. Oriental rugs cover the floors, and there are marble-topped dressers and tall walnut and oaken headboards in some rooms. One honeymoon suite has antique wicker and pink velvet.

Ornate iron furniture is set out on the porches for enjoyment by guests, who are free to explore the manicured grounds, lounge on the porches, or browse through the house. In the early morning the aroma of baking tea breads makes breakfast an irresistible temptation.

Accommodations: 4 rooms, 2 with private bath. *Driving Instructions:* Belle Aire is on Route 20 West.

MOTHER'S COUNTRY INN

349 Spring Street, Highway 20, Galena, IL 61036. 815-777-3153.
Innkeeper: Pat Laury. Open all year.

Mother's Country Inn is a classic brick townhouse built around 1838.
The inn's guest cottage, built in 1830, is Galena's oldest frame house,
now with housekeeping facilities, a wood-burning stove, and sleeping
facilities for six. The townhouse was restored by innkeeper Pat Laury
and opened as an inn in 1983. The seven guest rooms are furnished
with antiques, including some brass beds. There are quilts, braided
rugs, and yards of chintz, all set off by old pine floors, creating an
informal atmosphere. Amid this country comfort is central heating,
air conditioning and modern plumbing.

Guests get to know each other in the "antique shop," a sitting area
with a working fireplace or, on warm summer nights, on the screened
porch cooled by breezes from the hillside behind the inn. Mother's
Country Inn serves a Continental breakfast and is within walking distance of downtown Galena and just one block from the Galena River.

Accommodations: 7 rooms, 1 with private bath, and guest cottage.
Pets: Not permitted. *Driving Instructions:* The inn is one block west
of the bridge on Route 20 in downtown Galena.

THE VICTORIAN MANSION

301 South High Street, Galena, IL 61036. 815-777-0675. *Innkeeper:* Brig. Gen. (Ret.) Robert G. McClellan. Open all year.

The Victorian Mansion is a seventeen-room Italianate home built in 1861 by Augustus Estey, a wealthy lead smelter and banker. In the prosperous mining days the mansion was frequently the scene of parties that welcomed prestigious visitors to Galena, including Ulysses Grant. The Grant family reciprocated after their visit by having the Estey daughter spend the winter with them at the White House. Built on rock on a knoll overlooking Galena, the mansion has walls of 12-inch bricks, and the woodwork and fireplaces are original. There is a three-story brick coachhouse on the grounds, as well as the chimney and fireplace of an earlier building that served as the Estey home until the mansion was completed. The grounds include more than 2 acres of large shade trees.

As you enter the house, you pass a 10-foot-tall grandfather clock, which has clearance to spare, thanks to the high ceilings that are the rule in the mansion. Before you is the commanding oval staircase that spirals up to the third floor.

All guest rooms are on the second floor; three connect and once served as the master bedroom suite. Another was originally the nursery for the Estey family and is directly above the mansion's kitchen, where servants could hear the baby crying and come upstairs to comfort it. This room, which contains a brass bed, a marble-topped dresser and commode, and a love seat, is usually selected by honeymooning couples, of which an average of two a week come to the mansion. The room's large kerosene-lamp hanging chandelier, recently electrified, has yellow shades and is decorated with an intricate bird made of inlaid silver and green jewels. Hanging from the lamp are more than a hundred prisms. The walls in this room, as in all the guest rooms, are papered with Victorian prints set in "picture framing" with painted walls above. The other guest rooms have similar period lighting, some converted kerosene chandeliers and others converted gas lamps. Several rooms have heavy carved walnut bedroom sets that include 8-foot-6-inch–tall bedsteads with matching bureaus and commodes. Carpeting in the guest rooms is either original Oriental rugs or reproductions by Karastan. The woodwork throughout the mansion is hand-grained pine that was prepared to resemble oak trim and paneling.

Accommodations: 6 rooms; 1 with private bath, 5 sharing 2 baths. *Pets and children:* Not permitted. *Driving Instructions:* Take I-20 east from Dubuque or west from Rockford to the center of Galena.

Grand Detour, Illinois

Grand Detour, a sleepy little town in northwestern Illinois, is almost completely encircled by the Rock River. Early French trappers and traders in the area named the town for the oxbow bend in the river at this point. The Indians believed that the Rock River found the land here so beautiful that it turned back for a second look. In 1834 Grand Detour was settled by a Vermonter, Leonard Andrus, who saw the area's potential for development. It had water power and river transportation combined with the rich, fertile soil of the river valley. It had long been a favored spot for the Indians' gardens and hunting domain. The Vermonter and his fellow New Englanders mapped out the village and settled down. Two years later John Deere came to the town from Vermont, where fire had destroyed his shop. He soon learned that the pioneers' plow could not work well in the rich soil of the prairies, so he developed a steel plow that cleaned itself, which opened the West to agricultural development.

COLONIAL INN

8230 South Green St., Grand Detour, Dixon, IL 61021. 815-652-4422. *Innkeeper:* James W. Pufall. Open all year.

The Colonial Inn, built as a private residence by a local businessman, Solon Cumins, was constructed along classic Italianate lines. The big brick building was converted to a hotel before the turn of the century and remains so eighty years later. The adjoining estates are homes on spacious grounds. It is on 2 ½ acres of landscaped lawns shaded by many tall trees. The Colonial Inn is owned and run by James Pufall, who has augmented the remaining original furnishings of this Victorian estate with his own collection of antiques and near antiques. A visit to this inn and the town is like a trip back in time to the gracious era of the nineteenth century. The ground-floor rooms, including the parlor, have floor-to-ceiling windows shaded by the white-pillared porch. The furnishings and decor throughout the inn are primarily Victorian, with a smattering of earlier antiques. Most of the rooms have the original fireplaces, once the only sources of heat but now merely decorative.

Guest rooms are individually decorated in the styles of the period. Some are painted with the true Victorian colors, others have antique and reproduction wallpapers. Half the rooms have 12-foot ceilings, and the rest muddle through under 9-footers. Air-conditioning and private baths are available with some of the rooms. Although the night air is cool and fresh even in the hottest months, some people prefer air-conditioning. Be sure to say so if you are one of them. Three old-fashioned hall bathrooms are also provided.

Mr. Pufall offers sweet rolls or croissants in the morning. This is the only meal served.

Accommodations: 12 rooms, 4 with private bath. *Pets:* Not permitted. *Driving Instructions:* The inn is 5 miles north of Dixon off Route 2, and 35 miles south of Rockford off Route 2. Look for Rock Street in the village and go west three blocks. (Route 2 runs north and south.) The East-West Tollway, Route 5, is just below Dixon. Take Route 26 to Dixon and Route 2 at the arch north to Grand Detour.

Indiana

Indianapolis, Indiana

HOLLINGSWORTH HOUSE INN

6054 Hollingsworth Road, Indianapolis, IN 46254. 317-299-6700.

Innkeepers: Susan Muller and Ann Irvine. Open all year.

When the innkeepers found this 1833 farmhouse, it was in a sad state of repair, saved only from the wrecker's ball by a local historical society that included a member of the Hollingsworth family. Twelve miles from downtown Indianapolis, the inn is on 4 acres bordering a creek, adjoining an additional 120 acres under development as a recreational park.

Ann and Susan attended countless country auctions throughout the midwest in search of fixtures and furnishings. They reopened fireplaces, revealed and polished the original poplar floorboards, and hung wallpapers appropriate to the period. Fine china, antique sterling, and hand-woven antique linens are used in the breakfast room, and fluffy towels with lace trim and embroidered tablecloths transformed into curtains add to the decor. Guest rooms have antique beds with comforters or heirloom coverlets. The guest parlor, with Boston ferns in the windows, has upholstered chairs and a damask-covered sofa drawn up to the fireplace.

Accommodations: 5 rooms with private bath. *Pets and children:* Not permitted. *Driving Instructions:* The inn is in the northwest section of Indianapolis, just west of Georgetown Road and south of 62nd Street.

Middlebury, Indiana

PATCHWORK QUILT COUNTRY INN

11748 Country Road 2, Middlebury, IN 46540. 219-825-2417. *Innkeeper:* Arletta Lovejoy. Open all year except three weeks in February.

The Lovejoy family has owned and operated this 260-acre Amish-country farm for more than 100 years. About twenty-five years ago, the Lovejoys began began serving heartland dinners. Soon, as many as 100 diners were being served each evening, with dishes such as buttermilk-pecan chicken, burgundy steak, and herbed roast beef. These are followed by a dessert trolley with such choices as walnut torte, fresh fruit pies, German chocolate cake, and cheddar cheesecake.

A few lucky guests may stay overnight in one of the three old-fashioned guest rooms. One room, the Meadow, has an early-American cannonball bed with a miniature canopy and pale quilting. Another room with a canopied bed has a Franklin stove. Guests are also welcome to relax by the fireplace in the living room.

Accommodations: 3 rooms with shared bath. *Pets and children:* Not permitted. *Driving Instructions:* Take exit 107 from the Indiana Toll Road. Drive north on Route 13 to Route 2 and drive west 1 mile.

Mitchell, Indiana

Mitchell is the home of *Spring Mill State Park*, named for the picturesque stone mill built in 1816 that still stands in the restored *Pioneer Village* within the park boundaries. The mill creek, dam, and flume supply the water to turn the mill's 24-foot overshot waterwheel; it, in turn, drives wooden-geared millstones, which daily grind corn into meal that may be purchased by visitors. Surrounding the mill are a number of restored buildings that have survived from the early nineteenth century. Included are the village meeting house, apothecary shop, distillery, tavern, hat shop, mill office, spring house, and barn, as well as several pioneer dwellings. A shuttle bus conducts visitors from the Pioneer Village to stops at Spring Mill Lake, a Pioneer Cemetery, and two of the park's important caverns—*Donaldson Cave* and *Twin Caves*. Boat rides are offered on the underground rivers that flow through these caves and that are famous for their population of northern blindfish. The park is also the site of the Virgil Grissom Memorial, erected in honor of the Indiana astronaut.

SPRING MILL INN

Spring Mill State Park, Mitchell, Indiana. Mailing address: P.O. Box 68, Mitchell, IN 47446. 812-849-4081. *Innkeeper:* Wilhelmina Robinson. Open all year.

Spring Mill Inn is one of the finest state park inns that we know. The buff-colored building, constructed in 1939 of native limestone quarried in nearby Bedford, consists of a central three-story portion with wings fanning out on either side. The inn was fully remodeled in 1976, and the result is a blending of the traditional original building with some strikingly modern additions. One is a glass-walled conference room that looks out into the treetops through an angled window wall. Another is the unusual indoor-outdoor swimming pool whose two parts are connected by a moat under a glass wall. The inn's lounge combines red wall-to-wall carpeting, wood-paneled pillars, and a large limestone fireplace with comfortable wood and plaid upholstered furniture to provide a pleasant place to read, watch television, or just enjoy the fire.

The redecorated guest rooms have quality colonial reproduction furniture, color television, and telephones. Other inn facilities include a new two-story parking garage next to the inn, tennis courts, and horseback-riding stables. A game room off the pool is popular with the children of guests. The dining room at Spring Mill offers all three meals daily to both inn guests and daily visitors to the park. The standard à la carte dinner menu features the usual range of American foods. A daily special aimed to please all members of families staying at the inn might include beef stew over noodles, a complete spaghetti dinner, flounder, baked chicken, or ham and beans. The inn's special cornsticks, made from cornmeal ground at the mill in the park, are usually on the table. Hoosier hospitality and the opportunity to stay in this beautiful and historic park are two good reasons to plan a visit to Spring Mill Inn.

Accommodations: 75 rooms with private bath. *Pets:* Not permitted. *Driving Instructions:* Take Route 60 east from Mitchell to the park entrance.

New Harmony is a small town in the southwest corner of the state, about a half-hour's drive from Evansville. In 1814, Father George Rapp and his followers, separatists from the Lutheran Church, settled the area. In just ten years New Harmony was being hailed as a uniquely civilized and prosperous town in the wilderness. Then, in 1825, the separatists moved back East, selling the settlement to Robert Owen, a Welsh-born Scottish industrialist and social reformer. Owen established an early utopian community there, bringing with him scientists and educators. The community soon became one of the leading intellectual centers on the emerging Midwestern frontier.

Today, buildings remain from both the settlement and the utopian periods. Visitors should drop in at the *New Harmony Visitor Center* at North and Arthur streets or call 812-682-4474 for complete information about the ambitious restoration of New Harmony and about tours of the historic sites. The sites listed below are open 9 to 5 daily except where special hours are indicated. Admission is charged for a complete tour. The complete tour includes visits to the Atheneum and Theatrum, a modern structure designed by architect Richard Meier. There are five log structures at the corner of North and West streets displaying life in the early period. The five blockhouses have been re-erected on this site. Several houses of the period are open.

THE NEW HARMONY INN

North Street, New Harmony, Indiana. Mailing address: P.O. Box 581, New Harmony, IN 47631. 812-682-4491. *Innkeeper:* Gary J. Gerard. Open all year.

There is no historic country inn in or near New Harmony, but there is a brand new inn that is most intriguing. The New Harmony Inn, completed in 1974, consists of an "entry house" that serves as the reception and registration area and a separate building with guest rooms. The New Harmony area is filled with outstanding examples of contemporary architecture that, for the most part, blend harmoniously (pun intended) with the traditional buildings going back to the early nineteenth century. The New Harmony is a blend of traditional lines with strikingly modern interiors. The building that houses the guest rooms is a brick structure with modern single-paned windows and sev-

eral window-width balconies at the second-floor level. Many rooms have wood-burning fireplaces, and all have contemporary furnishings and decor that maintain the Indiana tradition of simplicity in line. Many have rush-seated rockers and desk chairs that, while new, reflect the heritage of Indiana furniture making. Some of the more expensive units consist of rooms with kitchenettes, living rooms, and spiral staircases that lead to sleeping "lofts." Within the entry house is a large, open-truss-roofed conference room as well as other seminar rooms that are frequently used for educational and business conferences and "retreats." A small chapel is available to guests for meditation. The inn has a "greenhouse" swimming pool available for swimming all year. No meals are served at the inn except breakfast, but the Red Geranium Restaurant is adjacent to the inn.

Accommodations: 45 rooms with private bath. *Pets:* Not permitted. *Driving Instructions:* New Harmony is 25 miles northwest of Evansville and is reached via Route 66, 68, or 69.

THE VICTORIAN HOUSE

Highway 231, Roachdale, Indiana. Mailing Address: R.R.1, Box 27, Roachdale, IN 46172. 317-522-1225. *Innkeepers:*Linda and Mark Ward-Bopp. Open all year except Christmas.

This Victorian was built in 1870 by Robert Bridges. When his seven children were grown, he gave each one eight acres, building houses positioned so that he could check up on them from his second-floor windows. The Victorian House was built from bricks kilned on the land and from black walnut, ash, and poplar cut from nearby woodlots. Its arched windows are trimmed by elaborate decorative moldings. The inn is decorated with period wallpaper, Oriental rugs, Victorian pieces, and lace curtains, and in winter there is usually a fire in the parlor hearth.

Linda Ward-Bopp offers special breakfast dishes such as apple puffs, apple-almond waffles, and eggs Benedict. Breakfast always includes fresh fruit and fresh-baked breads, rolls, or muffins.

Accommodations: 3 rooms with shared bath. *Driving Instructions:* The inn is on the west side of Route 231, about 13 miles north of Greencastle.

Michigan

Dearborn, Michigan

Dearborn is a city of 100,000 that houses one of the most important tourist attractions in the United States, *Greenfield Village*. Situated on 240 acres, the village is the largest collection of Americana in any one museum in the country. There are nearly a hundred significant or historic structures in Greenfield Village alone, and adjacent to it is the world-famous *Henry Ford Museum*.

Many buildings house year-round or seasonal demonstrations of early American crafts. Included in the year-round craft sereis are demonstrations of baking, blacksmithing, broom making, candle making, glassblowing, leatherworking, pewter working, pottery, silversmithing, spinning and weaving, and tinsmithing, among others.

THE DEARBORN INN

20301 Oakwood Boulevard, Dearborn, MI 48123. Toll-free: 800-221-7237 from Michigan, 800-221-7236 from elsewhere in the United States. *Innkeeper:* David Souther. Open all year.

The Dearborn Inn is a complex of lodgings built in 1931 by Henry Ford, with additions in 1960. Ford built the inn for the convenient accommodation of travelers who landed at the nearby Ford Airport. It was the first "airport hotel" and also served visitors to Ford's Greenfield Village and the Henry Ford Museum nearby. Accommodations are offered on the 23-acre site in three distinct life-styles: at the inn itself, in guest rooms in five reproduction colonial homes, and in two motor houses.

The inn reflects Ford's love for Georgian architecture in its imposing brick facade, which guests approach on a sweeping circular drive. The inn has a distinctly Southern feeling and appearance. Reproductions of many pieces of early American furniture are featured, as are carefully chosen wallpapers and paints that reflect the tints of the colonial period. The inn was fully air-conditioned in 1937, one of the first in the country to have this feature. With the repeal of Prohibition in the early 1930s, cocktail lounges were added to the nation's leading hotels. However, Ford was a strict teetotaler and would not permit their installation at the inn. Not until 1949, two years after his death, were a bar and cocktail lounge put into operation. The original inn offers overnight accommodations in ninety-four rooms.

In addition to rooms at the inn, visitors may choose rooms or suites in any of five colonial homes that are replicas of the homes of famous early Americans. Entrance halls, stairs, and sitting rooms are exact or close copies of the originals. The guest rooms have been slightly modified to accommodate modern conveniences such as private bathrooms. The furnishings of the homes are reproductions, in part, of pieces used in the original homes. The reproduction colonial houses offer a total of thirty-three rooms. There are also two motor houses for travelers who prefer facilities of this type.

For dining at the inn, the Early American Dining Room offers lunch and dinner, including a special seafood dinner on Fridays and brunch on Sundays. The pine-paneled Ten Eyck Tavern serves breakfast, lunch, and dinner from a moderately-priced menu.

Accommodations: 180 rooms with private bath. *Driving Instructions:* The inn is on Oakwood Boulevard. Take the Oakwood Boulevard exit off either I-94 or the Southfield Freeway (M-39).

Douglas, Michigan

ROSEMONT INN

83 Lakeshore Drive, Douglas, Michigan. Mailing address: P.O. Box 541, Douglas, MI 49406. 616-857-2637. *Innkeepers:* Ric and Cathy Gillette. Open all year, except mid-November through Christmas.

The Rosemont Inn is a turn-of-the-century Victorian resort hotel on the shore of Lake Michigan. The inn sits on a landscaped acre just 150 feet from the lake and about 75 feet above it. In most seasons there are panoramic vistas of the lake—except in summer, when the denseness of the trees partially obstructs the view.

The inn was owned by one family for eighty years. In 1982 Ric and Cathy Gillette bought the inn and completely restored and renovated it, installing country antiques to recapture the inn's early days and putting a modern bathroom in each guest room. The bedrooms are furnished with brass, four-poster, and canopied beds. The two public rooms feature game tables, television, and love seats and wing chairs grouped around fireplaces. The porches are decorated with Victorian gingerbread and are furnished with rocking chairs and love seats. The area containing the inn's heated swimming pool is landscaped with flowering bushes and other plants. In front of the inn old-fashioned street lamps have been electrified and add a soft glow to the night.

Accommodations: 14 rooms with private bath. *Pets:* Not permitted. *Driving Instructions:* Take the Douglas and Blue Star Highway to Center Street. Drive west on Center Street to Lake Michigan and then north on Lakeshore Drive 1/8 mile to the inn.

Homer, Michigan

GRIST GUEST HOUSE

310 E. Main Street, Homer, MI 49245. 517-568-4063. *Innkeeper:* Judith Krupka. Open all year.

Grist Guest House is an 11-room Colonial Revival with original natural oak woodwork, leaded-glass windows, and rooms decorated with antiques from the innkeeper's collection. The house was built in 1905 for the son of the town's miller, a Mr. Cortright. Guests have use of two sitting rooms, one a period piece from the turn of the century. Guests rooms are furnished with an eclectic blend of antiques. Breakfast is a three- or four-course meal set out on fine china, the food having a strong southern overtone. On Friday nights, Judith offers a package, including dinner and theater tickets. The inn is next door to a dinner theater that features Broadway shows six days a week. Nearby, visitors may tour the Kellogg's cereal factory at Battle Creek.

Accommodations: 6 rooms, 3 with private bath. *Pets and children:* Not encouraged. *Driving Instructions:* Take I-94 from Jackson, Michigan, to exit 136; drive 20 miles to Homer.

STUART AVENUE INN

405 Stuart Avenue, Kalamazoo, MI 49007. 616-342-0230. *Innkeepers:* Andrea and William Casteel. Open all year.

Little did Bill and Andy Casteel know just how demanding the task of renovating their 1889 Queen Anne–style Victorian would be. It took, for example, one full-time person and several helpers almost seven months just to strip all the woodwork in the house to its natural state. Then came weeks of painting and papering. The rewards, however, are self-evident. Take, for example, the Eastlake sitting room on the second floor. Furniture from the period gives the room its name, and light streams in from a large semicircular window that reaches from the floor almost to the ceiling. Downstairs, ten windows provide morning light in the breakfast room, where several round tables topped with lace and print cloths stand on a quarry-tile floor. Above, paddle fans turn lazily on warm summer mornings, while breakfast includes baked goods from Sarkozy's Bakery, homemade jams, and fresh fruit.

Each of the six guest rooms is named: The Arboretum, for example, is festooned with plants. Melinda's room, on the first floor, is perfect for honeymooning couples who enjoy its private entrance and fireplace. Outside, the inn's prize-winning, Victorian-style gardens are a perfect compliment to the decorative shingles and many gables. The inn is within walking distance of Kalamazoo College and not far from Western Michigan University, making it a popular spot for parents and friends visiting students.

Accommodations: 6 rooms with private bath. *Pets and children under 12:* Not permitted. *Smoking:* Not permitted. *Driving Instructions:* Take I-94 or Route 131 to Kalamazoo. The inn is at the northwest corner of Stuart and Kalamazoo avenues.

Lexington, Michigan

GOVERNOR'S INN

7277 Simons St., Lexington, Michigan. Mailing address: Box 471, Lexington, MI 48450. 313-359-5770. *Innkeepers:* Bob and Jane MacDonald. Open May through October.

The Governor's Inn is a big Victorian house just a short block from Lake Huron, taking advantage of the lake's cooling breezes. It was built in 1859 by Charles Moore, whose youngest daughter married Bert Sleeper in the summer of 1901. That fall her husband became a state senator and, in 1917, was elected governor. Governor's Inn was the Sleepers' retreat.

Jane and Bob MacDonald have transformed the retreat into an inviting bed-and-breakfast inn, complete with the old-fashioned charm of a turn-of-the-century summer house. There are rockers on the porch and wicker and country-style oak furniture throughout. The three guest rooms have iron beds and summer-style antique furnishings. A Continental breakfast is served.

There are many attractions within an easy stroll of the inn: The lake offers swimming, and a state-run marina is nearby. As a summer lakeside community, Lexington has many shops for exploring, and country auctions are the highlight of many summer weekends.

Accommodations: 3 rooms with private bath. *Pets:* Not permitted. *Children:* Under 12 not permitted. *Driving Instructions:* Take I-94 to Port Huron. Turn north on Route 25 to Lexington.

Mackinac Island is a summer resort island that has never really bowed to the twentieth century. Although it is easy to drive to, all cars must be left behind at Mackinaw City or Saint Ignace, from which ferries convey pedestrians to the island. Compared in its feeling to the British island of Bermuda, Mackinac Island, too, relies on horse and carriage and the bicycle to provide basic transportation. It is only 9 miles around and accessible to cyclists and hikers. Mackinac Island is steeped in history. The Jesuits made it the first outpost of civilization in the Northwest. During the American Revolution, the British built a fort on the island to supplement *Fort Michilimackinac.*

GRAND HOTEL

Mackinac Island, MI 49757. 906-847-3331; off season: 517-487-1800. *Innkeeper:* John M. Hulett III. Open mid-May through October.

The Grand Hotel is the Dowager Queen of Mackinac Island. This beauty, though nearly a hundred years old, is vibrantly alive today, gleaming white on a bluff high above the Straits of Mackinac where Lakes Huron and Michigan touch. She stands on 500 acres of landscaped grounds with flower gardens, groves of trees, woodlands, and acres of meticulously tended lawns and hedges.

The romance of the hotel begins the moment guests arrive on the island and step into the hotel's horse-drawn carriage. The horses are decked out in plumes, and the coachman wears a top hat and hunting pinks. The carriage brings guests right to the entrance, part of the hotel's most famous feature, its porch. Said to be the longest porch in the world, it has 880 feet of columns, fluttering American flags, bright yellow awnings, and flowers everywhere. Inside, the enormous parlor is a medley of bright colors, upholstered furnishings, softly lit chandeliers, and dark carpeting. There are wallpaper murals worthy of the spacious room, and vases of seasonal flowers and after-dinner concerts complete the picture.

The resort offers guests just about every service in a luxurious setting of another era. The large formal dining room, the parlor, and the guest rooms have all been remodeled in keeping with the splendid hotel and its special setting. The waters of the straits can be seen from

many parts of the hotel. Numerous public rooms offer guests relaxation, entertainment, cocktails, light meals, and dancing. Among the services and thoughtful touches here are complimentary morning coffee, evening demitasse in the parlor, concerts accompanying afternoon teas, and many resort activities, such as horseback riding on miles of trails and horse-drawn surrey tours of the island.

Most of the hotel's rooms have picture windows offering beautiful views. Each is decorated attractively in individual styles with bold colors in fabrics and wall coverings. Breakfast and dinner are included in the room tariff. The kitchen prides itself on the excellent Mackinac whitefish and aged prime rib of beef. The menu, which rotates every three nights, offers about ten entrées including fresh and smoked seafoods, roasts, steaks, and a number of more unusual choices that add variety and fun. The desserts are baked here, the specialty being the Grand pecan ball with fudge sauce.

The hotel first opened to guests in 1887 and was run under various owners virtually without profit for much of her life. She had many ups and downs; some of the downs nearly got her razed. Eventually she became the property of W. Stewart Woodfill, whose unflagging love and enthusiasm carried her through the Depression years. At one time during the Depression there were 411 employees on the payroll and only eleven paying guests. Mr. and Mrs. R.D. Musser, relatives of Mr. Woodfill, are the current owners.

Accommodations: 275 rooms with private bath. *Pets:* Not permitted. *Driving Instructions:* Ferries and airlines serve the island, which doesn't allow cars. The ferries run from Mackinaw City and from Saint Ignace on the mainland.

HOTEL IROQUOIS

Mackinac Island, MI 49757. 906-847-3321. *Innkeepers:* Sam and Margaret McIntire. Open mid-May to mid-October.

For those who feel overpowered by the Grand Hotel's size, the Iroquois is the perfect answer. Built as a private house at the turn of the century, it has been welcoming guests for more than seventy-five years. With time, it has grown in one direction and another but has managed to maintain the look and appeal of an earlier era. An addition completed for the 1980 summer season resulted in an enlarged dining room and an additional twelve guest rooms and suites. Some of these are in a newer tower and are among the most luxurious in the hotel.

For years the Iroquois has been content to be among the more expensive hotels on the island, safe in the knowledge that the standard it set would justify the price. The setting itself is worth some extra expense. The Iroquois is directly at the lakeshore, on a point of land, and the dining room and many of the guest rooms enjoy lake views. Particularly nice is dinner by candlelight, viewing the lake-freighters' far-off lights that flicker over the water. The hotel's Carriage House Dining Room offers a selection of chops, steaks, prime ribs, shrimp, lobster, and country-style baked chicken. A specialty is the Lake Superior whitefish. As many as twenty desserts are offered at dinnertime. These and all breads and rolls are prepared fresh daily by the hotel's full-time pastry chef.

Throughout the Iroquois the McIntires have maintained the look of a fine home with formal wallpapers, painted white trim, wall-to-

wall carpeting, and the highest quality hotel furnishings. Some guest rooms have cathedral ceilings, sitting rooms, or views from large bay windows. In warmer months guests can have cocktails outdoors overlooking the Straits of Mackinac, get a suntan on the hotel's sun deck, or sit quietly on the hotel's attractive round corner porch.

Accommodations: 47 rooms with private bath. *Pets:* Not permitted. *Driving Instructions:* Leave cars at Mackinaw City or Saint Ignace and take the ferry to the island. Alternatively, there is an air strip on the island for private airplanes.

THE NATIONAL HOUSE INN

102 South Parkview, Marshall, MI 49068. 616-781-7374. *Innkeeper:*
Barbara Bradley. Open all year except Christmas.

The National House is a perfect accompaniment to a village many
call the "Williamsburg of the Midwest." Built in 1835 as a stagecoach
stop, the inn has been fully restored, with modernization limited to
the installation of private bathrooms in all of the guest rooms. The
inn has been listed in the National Register of Historic Places and
is the oldest operating inn in the state.

Before the Civil War the inn reputedly was used as a stopover on
the Underground Railroad. The house continued to function as an
inn until 1878, when it was converted to a factory that produced
wagons and windmills. Just after the turn of the century, National
House was converted to apartments. It remained that way until its
purchase and restoration by the Kinney and Minick families. Finding
the property in a sadly neglected state, the new owners set about to
restore what could be restored and rebuild the remainder. In addition to installing private baths, the innkeepers built a brick fireplace
in the lobby, using bricks that had formerly blocked windows during
the apartment-house days. There is an additional fireplace in the
upstairs lounge that bears handsome paneling and, as in the rest of
the inn, a collection of early furniture. The unobtrusiveness of modern
conveniences at the National House Inn maintains the feeling of a
century and a half of history that pervades the inn. Furnishings are
varied and selected to match room by room. Thus the tone of the
upstairs lounge is set by the Windsor armchairs and early rockers,
while the Sidney Ketchum guest room is a Victorian masterpiece with
complementing carved massive bedstead and marble-topped, mirrored
dresser. Other guest rooms are set in the earlier period, their iron and
brass beds blending with early maple or pine furniture. Throughout,
the guest rooms have appropriate wallpapers that reproduce the small
prints popular before the twentieth century. Downstairs is a dining
room with salmon-colored woodwork, antique oak dining tables and
chairs, and a reproduction nineteenth-century folk-art hooked rug.
Also on this floor is a gift shop specializing in Victorian reproduction pieces. Throughout the inn are original Currier and Ives prints
selected to complement the early furnishings. In the morning, a Con-

tinental breakfast is served, the only meal offered. In pleasant weather the Victorian sitting garden is a restful gathering place that overlooks the centerpiece of Marshall, the Brooks Memorial Fountain.

The inn was at one time a popular stagecoach stop on the run between Detroit and Chicago. Today its proximity to I-94, the twentieth-century equivalent connecting the two great cities, means that the modern traveler can enjoy the same convenience in surroundings that are a good deal more comfortable than they were a century and a half ago.

Accommodations: 16 rooms with private bath (2 share a shower only). *Pets:* Not permitted. *Driving Instructions:* From I-94, use exit 110 and take old Route 27 south 1 1/2 miles to the inn. From I-69, exit at Michigan Avenue in Marshall and go straight 1 1/2 miles to the inn.

1873 MENDON COUNTRY INN

440 West Main Street, Mendon, MI 49072. 616-496-8132. *Innkeepers:* Jane and Lewis Kaiser. Open all year.

At the point where the Little Portage Creek meets the picturesque St. Joseph River stands the Mendon Country Inn. Mendon is a pretty little river town, and it has had an inn here since the late 1840s. Adam Wakeman built a new inn in 1873 after a fire had destroyed the original one. His Wakeman House was designed in an elegant post–Civil War fashion, with fanlights, high ceilings, arched windows, and a walnut circular staircase. After the Wakemans sold the hotel, it went into a steady decline under many owners until Jane and Lewis Kaiser rescued it in 1982. They spent an entire winter redoing the inn with a vast crew of workmen including Amish craftsmen and local young people.

The result is a restored inn with country-style rooms set off by rich Colonial colors, old-fashioned wallpapers, and the Kaisers' antiques. The Puddleburg Room honors the town's earlier name (sensibly changed to Mendon in the early nineteenth century), and it is here that guests gather for a breakfast of fruits and freshly baked pastries. Although this is the only meal served, the innkeepers can help guests choose a local restaurant.

Two guest rooms on the ground floor have private creekside porches. The Honeymoon Suite occupies the former Ladies Parlor and is the most romantic and elegant. On the first floor, the Nautical Room features rustic pine furnishings. A swag of fisherman's netting serves as the bed's canopy, and there is even a lobster pot. The wide halls are decorated with quilts and prints and have sitting areas where guests can relax and read or converse. Each guest room has antiques and decor appropriate to its theme—for example, Country Cousin, Amish, or Hired Man. A roof garden has a gazebo on its sun deck, with views of the surrounding woods and meadows and a creek with a fieldstone dam. A canoe livery is just behind the hotel, and guests can paddle down the creek or be portaged upriver for a day on the St. Joseph. The Kaisers provide 1940s bicycles for guests' use.

Accommodations: 11 rooms, 9 with private bath. *Pets:* Not permitted. *Children:* Under 13 not permitted. *Driving Instructions:* The inn is on Route 60, about halfway between Detroit and Chicago.

Port Sanilac, Michigan

THE RAYMOND HOUSE INN

111 South Ridge Street, Port Sanilac, MI 48469. 313-622-8800.
Innkeeper: Shirley Denison. Open May through October.

Port Sanilac in the scenic "thumb" area of Michigan was one of the original ports of call in the days when passenger steamers plied Lake Huron a century ago. The town has changed little since that time; sailors and power boaters are still attracted to the port. The Raymond House, a brick structure with intricate gingerbreading highlighting the exterior, was built here in 1871 for the prominent Raymond family and remained in their possession until Shirley Denison purchased the property in 1982. Shirley had summered in Port Sanilac with her grandfather since she was a child and had always loved the big house. The house needed little restoration, and her extensive collection of antiques was well suited to the large, high-ceilinged rooms. Shirley brought with her many skills, including art restoration, sculpting, and antique collecting. Her ceramic sculpture is displayed in the inn and is for sale, as are some of her antiques. A Continental breakfast including freshly baked rolls is served to guests.

Accommodations: 6 rooms with private bath. *Pets:* Not permitted. *Children:* Under twelve not permitted. *Driving Instructions:* Port Sanilac is 30 miles north of Port Huron on Route 25.

Saugatuck, Michigan

MAPLEWOOD HOTEL

   428 Butler Street, Saugatuck, Michigan. Mailing address: P.O. Box
1059, Saugatuck, MI 49453. 616-857-2788. *Innkeeper:* Donald Mitchell. Open all year.

The Maplewood, one of the grand old resort hotels, was built in the
heyday of Michigan's lumber boom in the mid-nineteenth century.
Opposite the village green, the Greek Revival hotel has been restored
to its 1860s splendor. Saugatuck, at the edge of Lakes Michigan and
Kalamazoo, has long been known as an artists' colony and boating
resort, offering year-round activities, including golf and cross-country
skiing. The town has many boutiques, galleries, and restaurants.

   A yellow Rolls Royce transports guests to and from the train station. The hotel's period decor features Queen Anne chairs, camelback
sofas, crystal chandeliers, and, in many guest rooms, fireplaces and
whirlpool baths big enough for two. A light Continental breakfast
is served in the dining room, and bar setups are available in a lounge
with a hearth and grand piano. A sun porch overlooks the town green.

   Accommodations: 12 rooms with private bath. *Driving Instructions:* From Chicago or South Bend, take I-94 to I-196. Take Exit
36 to Lake Street, which becomes Culver Street. Turn right on Butler.

THE PARK HOUSE

888 Holland Street, Saugatuck, MI 49453. 616-857-4535. *Innkeepers:* Lynda and Joe Petty. Open all year.

Park House, the oldest residence in Saugatuck, was built in 1857 by H.D. Moore, a wealthy lumberman who fenced his large yard so that his daughters could keep deer. The deer kept the lawns so tidy that townsfolk referred to the house as the Park House. It eventually fell into disrepair, until rescued in 1984 by Lynda and Joe Petty, who created a homey atmosphere with country antiques, print wallpaper, and hand stenciling.

Breakfasts of muffins and fresh coffee, fruits, and granola are served in the large, oak-decorated common room, where a wood-burning hearth adds atmosphere. A parlor has French doors that open out onto the yard, with its fountain and flower gardens. The front veranda is a good spot for warm-weather relaxing. The guest rooms, furnished with rocking chairs and brass beds, are color-coordinated with the private bathrooms. Park House is listed in the state historic register and in the National Register of Historic Places.

Accommodations: 7 rooms with private bath. *Pets:* Not permitted. *Children:* Under 12 not permitted. *Driving Instructions:* From Route 196, take exit 41 west. Follow the signs to Saugatuck business district. The inn is 1.9 miles on the right.

SINGAPORE COUNTRY INN

900 East Lake Street, Saugatuck, Michigan. Mailing address: P.O. Box 881, Saugatuck, MI 49453. 616-857-4346. *Innkeepers:* Michael and Denise Simcik. Open all year.

Two doves flying out of a red heart on the Singapore Country Inn's sign set the romantic tone for this turn-of-the-century lodging that overlooks Lake Kalamazoo. Inside, decorative tin ceilings, scrolly brass headboards, striped floral wallpapers, plush carpets, and coordinated comforters add to the mood. Each guest room has its own "tête-à-tête" sitting area. In addition, guests are welcome to use the common room and the veranda.

Formerly known as the Twin Gables Hotel, the inn was built about 1900 on the waterfront and later moved to its present site. In the 1920s it was purchased by Tom Carey, a vaudeville banjo player who performed at the Twin Gables frequently. In addition to its overnight guest accommodations, the inn has a country gift shop that specializes in local Michigan arts, crafts, and home-decorative items. A large Continental breakfast of melon or fruit, croissants, bagels, cream cheese, and coffee, tea, or hot chocolate is served to guests.

Accommodations: 8 rooms, all with private bath. *Pets:* Not permitted. *Children:* By prior arrangement only. *Driving Instructions:* Take I-196 to exit 36. Drive west 1 mile (on Blue Star Highway) and turn left on Lake Street.

WICKWOOD INN

510 Butler Street, Saugatuck, MI 49453. 616-857-1097. *Inn-keepers:* Sue and Stub Louis. Open all year.

The Wickwood Inn is a stately Federal-style home in the picturesque resort village of Saugatuck. Victorian homes dot the hills behind the busy harbor where the Kalamazoo River joins Lake Michigan. A graceful old ferryboat bedecked with gingerbread plies the waters just one block from the Wickwood Inn. The innkeepers, Sue and Stub Louis, enhance the British bed-and-breakfast flavor of their inn with tours of the village in their old London taxi.

A pair of handsome etched-glass doors in the entry set the mood of the inn. An airy living room features an antique Chinese rug in tones of navy and tan, which also make up the color scheme for the public rooms. The library has a mahogany bar where complimentary hors d'oeuvres are served with beer, wine, and soft drinks. A garden room has game tables with puzzles and cards, as well as wicker lounging chairs.

The guest rooms are furnished with antiques. Delicate Laura Ashley wallpapers and fabrics add old-fashioned romance throughout. A deluxe suite has a fireplace. Flower gardens surround the inn.

Accommodations: 10 rooms with private bath. *Pets and children:* Not permitted. *Driving Instructions:* Saugatuck is just off I-196 (exit 36 from the north or 41 from the south).

THE LAST RESORT—A BED AND BREAKFAST INN

86 N. Shore Drive, South Haven, MI 49090. 616-637-8943. *Inn-keepers:* Wayne and Mary Babcock. Open May through October. The Last Resort is on the historic North Beach peninsula overlooking South Haven's harbor and Lake Michigan. Contrary to its name, The Last Resort is believed to be one of the area's first resorts! The original house was built in 1883 by Civil War captain Barney Dyckman and was enlarged at the turn of the century when another building was moved to the site. The resort stood empty for almost twenty-five years before it was rescued and restored by Mary and Wayne Babcock. The rooms are furnished with antiques and decorated with local handicrafts. Each of the guest rooms, named for a ship built in South Haven, offers views of the lake and harbor and has an antique sink, but no private bath. A Continental breakfast is the only meal served.

The Babcocks are jewelry designers, and their work is displayed in the inn's gallery, which exhibits the work of regional artists as well. The grounds are landscaped with oaks and tall white pines, with a shady picnic area overlooking the lake.

Accommodations: 14 rooms with shared baths. *Pets and children under 12:* Not permitted. *Driving Instructions:* Take I-94 to I-196 north to South Haven; take exit 22 to North Shore Drive.

Union City, Michigan

THE VICTORIAN VILLA

601 North Broadway Street, Union City, MI 49094. 517-741-7383.

Innkeeper: Ron Gibson. Open all year.

William P. Hurd served the Union City area as a "saddle bag" doctor from 1840 until he retired in 1865 to direct the Union City National Bank. In 1876 Hurd completed his high-Victorian Italianate house for the then princely sum of $12,000. "Doc Billy" died in 1881 after living in his dream house for only five years. His widow, Caroline, lived in the villa until her death in 1910 at the age of eighty-nine.

The innkeeper has decorated his inn to reflect the decades of the late nineteenth century. Thus guests may choose from the 1850s Empire Room, the 1860s Rococo Room, the 1870s Renaissance Room, the 1880s Eastlake Room, and the country-Victorian Tower Suite. The last, a favorite with romantics, features a tower sitting room and a private bath.

A nice feature of the Victorian Villa is its afternoon tea, with brimming cups of English tea served with all the trimmings. Breakfast at the inn includes fruit, home-baked Amish and European pastries with Amish cheese and boiled eggs. At bedtime the innkeeper places fancy chocolates on the pillow of each guest.

Accommodations: 8 rooms, 6 with private bath. *Pets and smoking:* Not permitted. *Driving Instructions:* Take I-69 15 miles south from Marshall to Rt. 60. Drive 7 miles west on Rt. 60 to Union City.

Minnesota

Chaska, Minnesota

BLUFF CREEK INN

1161 Bluff Creek Drive, Chaska, MN 55318. 612-445-2735. *Innkeeper:* Marjorie Bush. Open all year except Thanksgiving Day and Christmas Eve.

Bluff Creek Inn has deer feeding in the yard, lace curtains, and country breakfasts on antique china, silver, and crystal. The farmhouse sits on land granted by Abe Lincoln to one of the earliest settlers of this area, who built the house in 1880.

Marjorie Bush provides late afternoon wines and mulled cider with fondues or snacks. In warm weather guests gather on the kitchen porch as the sun sets. There is an antique stove in the Victorian parlor. Rooms have been restored with family antiques, quilts, and Victorian pieces, all highlighted by designer fabrics and English garden wallpapers. The inn is ten minutes from a restored nineteenth-century village and the Minnesota Renaissance Festival. Minneapolis is 15 miles away.

Accommodations: 4 rooms, 1 with private bath, 3 with half bath. *Pets and children:* Not permitted. *Driving Instructions:* From the junction of Routes 101 and 212 in Shakopee, turn west onto Route 212. The inn is 1 mile from Shakopee.

Duluth, Minnesota

THE MANSION

3600 London Road, Duluth, MN 55804. 218-724-0739. *Innkeeper:* Susan Monson. Open mid-May–mid-October and all weekends. The Mansion is a twenty-five-room Tudor-style estate built in 1929. Guests can poke about in the rooms, nooks, and crannies, or take part in the house tours offered each morning after breakfast. Each of the nine guest rooms is different, and one has a working fireplace. The Mansion is reflected in the lake just outside its front door and is surrounded by six acres of well-tended grounds, including formal gardens, lawns, a carriage house, and 500 feet of beachfront on Lake Superior. Just three blocks away is another mansion, Glensheen, which is also open to the public for tours. Although breakfast is the only meal served, there are a number of restaurants nearby.

Accommodations: 9 rooms, 4 with private bath. *Pets:* Not permitted. *Driving Instructions:* From downtown Duluth, take Route 61 (London Road) about 5 miles east.

Grand Marais, Minnesota

CASCADE LODGE

Box 693, Route 61, Grand Marais, MN 55604. 218-387-1112. *Innkeepers:* Gene and Laurene Glader. Open all year.

Cascade Lodge, a clapboard-over-log and stone building, is separated only by Route 61 from the rockbound coast of Lake Superior. Built in the 1930s, the lodge has grown and been modernized over the years but has consistently resisted the chrome and plastic look that befell many of its competitors. The 1980s Cascade Lodge consists of the main building with its guest rooms, a detached restaurant in a similar architectural style, a small motel unit, and nine guest cabins. Behind the buildings stretches a seemingly endless aspen forest laced with hiking trails that become cross-country skiing trails at the first snowfall.

The Gladers have maintained the feeling of home throughout the lodge and cabins. Rooms are varied; those in the lodge have plaster walls, carpeting, and hot-water heating. Some of the cabins are built of logs and retain their natural log-wall interiors, while others have painted or paneled walls. Each guest room, regardless of location, has its own modern bathroom.

The Fireplace Room at the lodge is dominated by its radial-beam ceiling. There are a natural-stone fireplace, a picture window overlooking Lake Superior, and comfortable furnishings that invite guests to linger and relax. Opening off this room through a triple door is another room with a picture window facing the lake, a grand piano, television, a game table, desks, and comfortable sofas and chairs. A large collection of trophy animal mounts and skins including those of timber wolves, moose, bear, coyote, geese, and fish decorate the lounges and the dining room.

The restaurant, also overlooking the lake, has a large menu with about fifteen fish and seafood offerings and an equal number of meat and poultry dishes. House specialties include Lake Superior trout, barbecued ribs, and charcoal-broiled steaks. Many guests ask especially for the barbecued chicken wings offered as an appetizer, or for the whole "deep browned" potatoes made according to a secret recipe.

In winter the focus of activity at the lodge is its excellent 32-mile cross-country ski trail system, which connects with an additional 130 miles of groomed trails of the North Shore Trail system. Snowshoeing is also popular, and photographers often capture the antics of the semitame deer that come to the lodge to eat food set out for them. In summer, Cascade Creek flows between the cabins to the lake; several hiking trails wind back between the creek and the river to Lookout Mountain. The Cascade Creek Nature Trail has been laid out with thirty-one numbered stopping places so guests can inspect firsthand the flora and fauna of the surrounding woodland. The lodge will be happy to furnish a guide for those who want to find the best local fishing spots. Families traveling with children will be pleased with the number of games, crafts, and planned activities at the lodge.

Accommodations: 13 rooms in main lodge, a 4-unit motel, and 9 cabins, all with private bath. *Pets:* Permitted in cabins only. *Driving Instructions:* The lodge is 9 miles southwest of Grand Marais on Route 61.

GUNFLINT LODGE

Gunflint Trail, Grand Marais, Minnesota. Mailing address: P.O. Box 100 GT-C1, Grand Marais, MN 55604. Toll-free: 800-328-3362 from Minnesota, 800-328-3325 from elsewhere in the United States. *Innkeepers:* Bruce and Sue Kerfoot. Open mid-May through mid-October and late December through March 31.

Gunflint Lake, at an elevation of 1,543 feet, lies along the Canadian border 43 miles inland from the Lake Superior shore at Grand Marais. Here, the Kerfoot family has been welcoming guests to their lodge for more than fifty years. First opened in 1928, the lodge complex has grown almost every year. There are eighteen cabins, four suites in the Trading Post building, two chalets, a sauna, and the main lodge. Fully developed family recreational activities include a children's playground, badminton, shuffleboard, tennis, and a marina offering boating, waterskiing, lake fishing, and a swimming raft. The surrounding woods have a network of hiking trails. The Gunflint Northwoods Outfitters, with headquarters on the property, organized canoe trips throughout the surrounding million-acre Boundary Waters Wilderness Area.

Accommodations vary in architectural style from rustic log cabins to frame clapboard buildings to earth-shelter units. Most have fireplaces and are pine-paneled. Cabins range in size from one to four bedrooms and are furnished with linen and towels. Furniture tends to be modern in the guest cabins, most of which have supplementary electric heat. Some rooms have private saunas and whirlpool baths.

Gunflint's main lodge is a rustic building with a trussed roof having exposed heavy beams; it has polished hardwood floors with braided area rugs and upholstered casual redwood furniture. One wall consists of a native-stone fireplace and large picture windows overlooking the lake and the Canadian shore in the distance. Another wall is a library corner filled with books; still another has card tables where guests often gather for bridge. Next to the lounge is the dining room, where back-country log chairs are drawn up to pine tables. Here, too, a fire burns on cool days.

The lodge serves a variety of home-cooked meals. Typical breakfasts include fresh fruit juice (a luxury this far from city life), cereals, pancakes, eggs, French toast, and bacon or sausage. The choice at lunch is usually between a hot dish like chicken à la king and a cold plate or sandwiches. The lodge will pack picnic lunches for guests who want to spend the day on the lake. Dinners feature, besides meats and vegetables, freshly made soups, breads, and desserts. On most summer Sundays the lodge has a lavish smorgasbord that attracts diners from miles around. Monday evenings traditionally offer spaghetti and pizza dinners, and there is often a midweek outdoor barbecue.

One of the special features of Gunflint Lodge is its strong naturalist program. Each week the several resident staff members lead activities from a list of more than thirty, including outings to study a beaver colony, a magnetic-rock trip, and a wildflower-identification trip. Indoor activities include candlemaking, rock tumbling, and wreath making. Because of this, the lodge has become particularly popular with families traveling together. Children frequently remain in camp while their parents enjoy north-country fishing for walleye, lake trout, bass, or northern.

Accommodations: 24 rooms or suites in cabins or chalets, all with private bath. *Driving Instructions:* Take U.S. 61 to Grand Marais; then head inland for 44 miles along the Gunflint Trail (Route 12) to the lodge.

Lake City, Minnesota

THE RAHILLY HOUSE

304 Oak Street, Lake City, MN 55041. 612-345-4664. *Innkeepers:* Mark and Denise Peters. Open all year.

Lake City, which lays claim to being the birthplace of water skiing, is nestled on the shore of Lake Pepin, the widest point on the Mississippi River, now the focus of all manner of water sports, boating, and fishing. In 1868, the town's first postmaster built a handsome, columned Greek Revival home where he and his wife resided for many years. Later, the home was purchased by Mr. Patrick Rahilly, an Irish immigrant who went on to become a state senator.

Today, Rahilly House offers antique-filled guest rooms, including three with fireplaces. Throughout the house, quarter-sawed oak floors gleam. The inn's dining room seats sixteen for a traditional, full country breakfast, while the parlor, with its gray marble fireplace, is a popular place for guests and the innkeepers to gather.

Accommodations: 7 rooms, one with private bath. *Pets:* Not permitted. *Children:* Under twelve not permitted. *Driving Instructions:* Take Route 61 along the river to the center of Lake City and Lyon Street. Drive two blocks southeast to Oak Street and turn left. The inn is at the corner of Marion Street.

MRS. B's HISTORIC LANESBORO INN

101 Parkway, Lanesboro, MN 55949. 507-467-2154. *Innkeepers:* Jack and Nancy Bratrud. Open all year.

Mrs. B's was built of native limestone in 1872, and for the next century it served as a furniture store and mortuary. The exterior retains its original stone facing, but the interior has been completely restored to suit its new purpose. Downstairs, the lobby has a library, grand piano, and a sweeping staircase leading to the guest rooms above. The dining room serves breakfast and lunch to guests and dinner to the public as well. Dinner specialties include ginger pork roast with fruit, Root River baked trout with wild-rice pilaf, and special holiday dinners that highlight a particular ethnic tradition.

Each of the nine guest rooms has a bath, a queen-size bed, wing chairs, a desk, and reading materials. Several open onto decks on the two upper floors. In choosing decorations, the Bratrud's paid homage to the area's Norwegian settlers. One room has a built-in bed trimmed with *rosemal*, the traditional Norwegian rose painting, and is surrounded with drawn curtains making it a *skanpseng*, or "cupboard bed." Three other rooms have *himmelseng*, or "heavenly beds," as canopied four-poster beds are called in Norwegian. Chocolate kisses, sherry, fresh flowers, and fruit are all part of the amenities, with champagne for anniversaries and other special occasions.

Accommodations: 9 rooms with private bath. *Pets:* Not permitted. *Driving Instructions:* The inn is on Route 16.

New Prague, Minnesota

New Prague is a small farming community enriched by its large Czechoslovakian and German populations. Nearby are an eighteen-hole golf course, tennis courts at local parks, and cross-country skiing on the Minnesota Valley Ski Trail. Fishing is available at Cedar lake; the Minnesota River just 9 miles away is a popular canoeing spot.

SCHUMACHER'S NEW PRAGUE HOTEL

212 West Main Street, New Prague, MN 56071. 612-758-2133 (Metro: 612-445-7285). *Innkeeper:* John Schumacher. Open all year except December 24 to 26.

When John Schumacher first discovered New Prague in 1974, he fell in love with both the Czechoslovakian and German town and its small hotel. Built in 1898 to a design by Cass Gilbert, the architect of the Minnesota state capitol, the hotel desperately needed a complete renovation. John realized that here was the framework with which to realize his dream of creating a country inn serving superb food. This dream has come true.

The inn clearly set out to cater to sentimentalists of all ages. It has flowery canopied beds, quilted comforters and down pillows. There are antique chests with painted panels, claw-footed tubs with flowered sides and pierced-heart–back chairs. Each room is named for a month of the year, the name proclaimed on unusual painted medallions above each door. Imported from Munich, the "Oktober" medallion, for example, shows a Bavarian farmer sowing his fields. The deep mulberry color of the room is highlighted with hand-painted pink chrysanthemums. Imported Bavarian lamps, an Austrian tablecloth, Persian rugs, and tapestry hangings combine with a dark, antique-finished double bed to carry out the hotel's European theme. In the "Mai" room, the canopy bed is so high that a small ladder has been installed to provide easy access. The storybook design over the bed pictures life from newlywed to old age. The "August" room has a primitive red-heart stencil design on the floors, a theme that extends to chairs and table. The rooms for every month are captivating in spirit and decor.

Because the hotel is a comfortable drive from the metropolian area, many guests come out specifically to sample the very special cuisine. The hotel's executive chef, John has researched his extensive menu with care and created dishes that reflect the town's Czech and German traditions, a distinctly French influence, and a touch of regional Minnesota. John's specialties are his quail stuffed with plums, pheasant in cream with mushrooms and shallots, roast duck the Czech way with caraway seeds, and several types of schnitzel.

Big Cally's Bar is named for John's father, Carlton Schumacher. One can sit at the antique marble bar on unusual wooden stools with hand-carved "boot" feet. Czech and German beers and a variety of cocktails are served in this room, which is presided over by a carved wooden Bavarian friar, imported from Germany. This room is just one more reason to go out of your way to stay in New Prague.

Accommodations: 12 rooms with private bath. *Pets:* Not permitted. *Children:* Not encouraged. *Driving Instructions:* From Minneapolis, take Route 35W South to Route 13 South. Go through Savage and Prior Lake, staying on Route 13 until it meets Route 19 west. Take this into New Prague (about 50 miles from the metropolitan area).

PRATT-TABER INN

706 West 4th Street, Red Wing, MN 55066. 612-388-5945. *Innkeepers:* Jane and Charles Walker and Jan and Darrell Molander. Open all year.

The Pratt-Taber Inn is a restored 1876 Victorian that combines a homey atmosphere with formal furniture and decorative arts of the period. In the public rooms, heavy swagged curtains hang at the windows, and Oriental rugs and tufted furniture in rich greens and reds are the rule. In the guest rooms, mirrored marble-top Victorian dressers, lace bedspreads on high-back Victorian beds, and period lighting fixtures maintain the atmosphere. Upstairs, Polly's Room has a nine-foot-high mid-Victorian dresser and a queen-size brass bed. The black marble fireplace is in contrast to the soft blue and ecru decor. Henrietta's Room has an 1865 triple-paneled double bed with fruit and nut cresting. A side door leads to an open deck perfect for watching the stars. Breakfast is the only meal served, but guests can easily explore downtown, either by foot, by car, or by trolley or horse and buggy, which will pick up guests for tours of the city.

Accommodations: 6 rooms, 2 with private bath. *Driving Instructions:* From St. Paul, take Route 61 south along the Mississippi River to Red Wing.

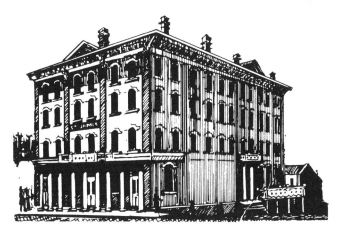

ST. JAMES HOTEL

406 Main Street, Red Wing, Minnesota. Mailing address: P.O. Box 71, Red Wing, MN 55066. 612-388-2846. *Innkeeper:* E. F. Foster. Open all year.

Built in 1875, the St. James Hotel was the subject of a major renovation several years ago, and it may now be counted among the finest Victorian-hotel restorations in the Midwest. A great deal of the credit for this restoration must be given to decorator Carol Bloomberg. It was her goal to make the St. James a living museum of the Victorian period. Each of its forty-one original guest rooms contains at least one antique piece. Most of the room lighting consists of the hotel's original gas fixtures, which were electrified. Where Carol was unable to find a suitable antique, she had an appropriate period reproduction made.

Before the restoration, there were sixty rooms in the hotel and but two bathrooms on each floor. By reducing the number of rooms, a private bathroom could be installed for each guest room. Carol's efforts at re-creating the Victorian period included reinstating wall bordering so characteristic of that time. Then coordinated wallpapers were chosen, and handmade quilts were ordered from quilt makers in the Twin Cities. Carol skillfully hid television sets in the rooms' cabinetry; so the twentieth century does not intrude too forcefully. A nice touch is the children's play area underneath the stairway on the third floor. There a collection of antique toys and reproductions of early playthings has been assembled.

The St. James's historic lobby was completely redecorated during the restoration. Its front desk is the original one, which has served registering guests for more than a century. The grand staircase goes to the second floor and is a favorite subject for photographers. Just off the lobby is the hotel's library. There a fire is usually burning in the fireplace, and guests may sit before it and enjoy a drink ordered from the bar.

The Port of Red Wing restaurant serves lunch and dinner seven days a week. A part of the original hotel, it was built of limestone carved from the bluffs that surround the town. The Victorian Dining Room is open Wednesday through Saturday, offering Continental dishes in a more formal setting.

The hotel offers views of the Mississippi River, just across Levee Park. From May through mid-October the *City of Red Wing*, one of the last wooden passenger boats operating on the Mississippi River, is used for two-hour sightseeing cruises. The Red Wing Heritage Preservation Commission prepared an excellent walking and driving tour of this historic riverfront town that includes a description of most of the historic buildings in Red Wing.

Accommodations: 60 rooms with private bath. *Pets:* Not permitted. *Driving Instructions:* Take Route 61 into Red Wing. The hotel is on the corner of Bush and Main streets.

Rochester, Minnesota

CANTERBURY INN BED AND BREAKFAST

723 Second Street SW, Rochester, MN 55901. 507-289-5553. *Innkeepers:* Mary Martin and Jeffrey Van Zant. Open all year.

The innkeepers of this 1890 Victorian inn are two women who offer guests a great deal more than just room and board in a pleasant setting. The innkeepers came from careers in nursing and church work and truly enjoy their new profession. The Canterbury Inn is just a few blocks from the Mayo Clinic and St. Mary's Hospital. Mary and Jeffrey bring warmth and enthusiasm to their inn and offer a home away from home to clinic visitors and patients' families as well as vacationers and business travelers.

The innkeepers restored the house, which has intricate woodwork, stained glass, and many gables. They did much of the work themselves and joked that they didn't really need sandpaper; they could have used their bare hands. Today guests enjoy joining the innkeepers by the fireside in the parlor for hors d'oeuvres and afternoon tea. They are served full breakfasts in the dining room or in their own rooms on request. There are homemade breads and wonderful entrées such as Grand Marnier French toast and pesto omelets. Each bedroom is decorated with antiques and contains quilts, lace-trimmed dresser scarves, and Victorian mementos. One headboard was created out of an ornate door found in the house.

Accommodations: Four rooms with private bath. *Pets:* Not permitted. *Driving Instructions:* Take U.S. 52 south from Minneapolis–St. Paul. Exit at Second Street SW and drive about seven blocks east.

Sauk Centre, Minnesota

PALMER HOUSE HOTEL

500 Sinclair Lewis Avenue, Sauk Centre, MN 56378. 612-352-3431.

Innkeepers: R. J. Schwartz and Al Tingley. Open all year.

For many years, the old Sauk Centre House stood on a corner of Main Street. Although the building was serviceable, most of the local residents felt that it had outlived its usefulness, and they longed for a really first-class hotel. Then, in 1900, it burned to the ground, paving the way for the construction of the Palmer House by Richard L. Palmer two years later. The resulting three-story brick hotel with curved-arch, stained-glass windows on the street level satisfied the townspeople and served the community well for the next quarter century or so.

One later-to-be-distinguished employee in this heyday period at the Palmer House was Sinclair Lewis. While in high school he worked at the hotel for spending money. But his personal distinction did not, apparently, include an aptitude for hotel work. He was an exasperation to the management and was finally fired for daydreaming. Later

Lewis would use his experiences at the Palmer House as a basis for his novel *Work of Art.*

By the mid-1920s the railroad began to be supplanted by the automobile as the main means of transportation, and business at Palmer House dwindled. By the time Al Tingley and Richard Schwartz discovered the place, it was sadly in need of repairs.

Friends since college days, the current owners bought the hotel in 1974, using some of the profits realized from an earlier restoration of a mansion in Saint Paul. At first, the project almost overwhelmed them, because they had to replace part of the roof, redo the plumbing and electrical systems, and then proceed from room to room to restore the hotel to its original state. Although the hotel has many handsome features, it never was regarded as having Victorian elegance. Instead, it had been designed to provide comfort to the legions of "drummers" (traveling salesmen) who passed through with their sample cases bulging with goods to be sold to the local merchants. When the new owners took over, the original features from the traveling-salesman era survived intact but had been hidden. The original tin ceiling in the lobby and the curved stained-glass windows had only to be re-exposed. Their efforts led to the hotel's designation as a state and national historic site. Al has recently written a book, available for purchase at the hotel, about his experiences as an innkeeper.

Many of the hotel's restored guest rooms have such original furnishings as the writing desks, chairs and beds. Floral prints on the walls, electrified wall sconces, and chenille bedspreads hark back to the earlier period. Rooms without a bath have a wall sink, a step up from the even earlier bowl and pitcher of cold water.

The Palmer House Restaurant serves three meals a day to guests and the public. The restaurant serves typically Midwestern "home cooking" that features steaks, roast beef and pork, fried ham, country-style ribs, baked or fried chicken and dressing, and chicken Pauline (baked in a wine sauce). Specials often include Cornish game hen, Hawaiian chicken, beef in burgundy, and shishkabob.

Accommodations: 37 rooms, 4 with private bath. *Driving Instructions:* Sauk Centre is halfway between the twin cities and Fargo, North Dakota, on I-94 and Highway 71.

COUNTRY BED AND BREAKFAST

32030 Ranch Trail, Shafer, MN 55074. 612-257-4773. *Innkeepers:* Lois and Budd Barott. Open all year.

Shafer is in a region settled by Swedish immigrants during the last half of the nineteenth century. Country Bed and Breakfast is a tidy red-brick home built in the 1880s by one of these immigrants. The Barotts are of Swedish descent, still speak the language, and enjoy many of the Swedish traditions strongly held by their neighbors. Shafer is still farm country, and one can drift off to sleep at the Barott's with the expectation that the first sounds one will hear in the morning will be the crowing of their three roosters. Later one is likely to be served eggs from the innkeepers own chickens and muffins or bread topped with honey from Budd's hives. The Barott's tap their own maple trees and make the syrup that appears on Lois' special-recipe buttermilk pancakes. Lois often serves fruit from their own garden, and she still brews her coffee by the "Swedish Egg" method.

The Barott's B&B has a white-pillared front porch that overlooks a lawn dotted with birches, maples, and mountain ashes. Within, their B&B has antiques that were inherited from their parents and grandparents. Bedrooms are wallpapered, have light and airy curtains, and include wicker or antique furniture. Homemade comforters grace the beds. An attic room has been renovated to accommodate a lounge area for guests and a bathroom. Downstairs, a wood-burning stove in the kitchen adds its warmth during the winter months.

Accommodations: 3 rooms with shared bath. *Pets:* Not permitted. *Children:* 12 and over permitted. *Smoking:* Not permitted. *Driving Instructions:* Take Route 21 north through Shafer. Go 1 1/2 miles to Ranch Trail, turn left; the inn is the second house on the left.

Stillwater, Minnesota

Stillwater has been called the birthplace of Minnesota because a convention was held here in 1838 to organize the Minnesota Territory.

LOWELL INN

102 North Second Street, Stillwater, MN 55082. 612-439-1100.
Innkeepers: Arthur and Maureen Palmer. Open all year.

The Lowell Inn, an imposing brick hotel, stands on the corner formerly occupied by the Sawyer House, which was built in 1848 and succumbed to the wrecker's ball in 1924. Completed six years later, the Lowell opened its doors on Christmas Day to serve its first meal. The inn was the dream of Nelle and Arthur Palmer, Sr. Both had spent much of their youth on the road—she as an actress and he as a pianist. Their traveling life showed them how often hostelries missed the mark and gave them an ambition to do the job right. They did not actually own the inn but served as managers for the owner, Elmore Lowell. The Palmers set out to fill the inn with a collection of fine antiques, augmented by the best linens, furniture, and other accoutrements of the hotel trade they could find. In 1945 the Palmers finally realized their lifelong dream and purchased the inn. In time they were joined by their children in the innkeeping business, as the Lowell continued to prosper. Arthur, Sr., died in 1951 and Nelle in 1970, but the tradition of excellence established by the parents is carried on by Arthur, Jr., and Maureen.

The inn comprises guest rooms and several dining rooms housed in a Williamsburg-style brick building dominated on the street side by a full-length veranda, the roof of which is supported by thirteen two-story columns. Within the inn are three dining rooms, each quite different from the others. The George Washington, the first of the dining rooms, was opened by Nelle Palmer in 1930. It has Capo di Monte porcelains, Sheffield silver services, and a Dresden china collection displayed on the sideboards about the room. Ladderback chairs in the Williamsburg style and portraits of George and Martha Washington help set the colonial style. In 1939, Arthur, Sr., decided to build a second dining room with an outdoor trout pool from which guests could select their own trout dinner. When the natural springs in the adjoining hillside began to seep into the new room, Arthur decided to move the pool indoors and make it a centerpiece of the décor. The menu served in these two dining rooms varies somewhat from weekdays to Sundays but generally includes broiled chicken with country gravy, lamb chops, chicken livers with morelles sauce, fresh brook trout, fillet of pike, filet mignon, sirloin steak, fried shrimp, and several other selections. The dinner menu has received acclaim from the day the restaurant opened.

The lobby and the guest rooms on the two upper floors reflect the love of Nelle and Arthur, Sr., for the French provincial, combined with the mood of Williamsburg. Some rooms have been recently redecorated with hand-carved Mexican sinks, whirlpool baths, thick carpeting, and overstuffed sofas. Most of the others retain the colonial antiques and complementing decorations established by the Palmers over many years.

Accommodations: 20 rooms with private bath. *Pets:* Not permitted. *Driving Instructions:* From Saint Paul take Route 36 east. Route 36 becomes Main Street in Stillwater. Turn left at the second light onto Myrtle and go one block to Second Street. Turn right, and the inn is on the corner.

Wabasha, Minnesota

THE ANDERSON HOUSE

333 West Main Street, Wabasha, MN 55981. 612-565-4524. *Innkeepers:* Jeanne, John, and Gayla Hall. Open every day of the year except Christmas.

If one were to ask a fancier of country inns what he or she looked for in an inn, the list would probably include warm, congenial, experienced innkeepers; a quiet setting, perhaps overlooking a river; original antique furnishings in a historic building; a friendly house cat or two; some hot bricks to warm chilly sheets in a quilt-covered bed; and lots of good country cooking with perhaps more than one or two kinds of fragrant home-baked breads.

Such a connoisseur certainly will not be disappointed at the Anderson House in Wabasha, Minnesota, which meets all the above requirements and offers much more. As Minnesota's oldest operating hotel, it is in the National Register of Historic Places. It has been in continuous service to hungry and weary travelers since its opening in 1856 and has been in the same family for four—"going on five"—generations.

The brick hotel overlooks the Mississippi River in the residential section of Wabasha, which has large yards, gardens, and flowers everywhere. The entry hall is a spacious lobby. Ida's Old Fashioned Ice Cream Parlor has been installed in one corner of the huge room. The Writing Room off the lobby, which has been converted to an antique shop, sells antique glassware as well as local arts and crafts. It is run by Johanna Hall, with the apparent moral support of a myna bird named Jimmy. A bevy of cats make up the rest of the Anderson House menagerie. While guests pamper the cats, they themselves are pampered by the Halls and their staff. There are hot bricks to warm the beds and mustard plasters if one feels a chill coming on; dusty shoes left outside the bedroom door at night return bright and shiny the next morning.

The Anderson House's guest bedrooms include a few in house-keeping cottages in back of the hotel. Each room has a different wallpaper, and hand-made quilts pick up the colors of the walls. The quilts are either antique or hand-sewn by two ladies in the Wabasha Nursing Home. The beds, bureaus, and night tables are curly maple, dark mahogany, and rich walnut. There are elaborate settees, cushioned Victorian chairs, and marble-topped dressers in rooms looking out over the Mississippi and the inn's gardens. Many rooms have private baths, and the remainder share old-fashioned hall bathrooms.

Downstairs, guests will find some of the best Pennsylvania Dutch cooking outside of Lancaster County, Pennsylvania. Although not all the cooking is "plain people's food," it certainly is the main attraction. Grandma Ida Anderson learned her cooking skills at her mother's side in Pennsylvania before coming to Minnesota. For breakfast, guests are offered cinnamon rolls and hot sticky buns, home-cured ham, cornmeal mush, red flannel hash, eggs, scrapple, and doughnuts. Other meals are no less impressive. Favorite soups are Pennsylvania Dutch chicken corn chowder, bacon corn chowder, Dutch beer and cheese soup, and a chicken soup with homemade noodles. Entrées include chicken with Dutch dumplings, deep-dish chicken pies with butter crusts, smoked stuffed pork chops served with a special braised red cabbage, pork tenderloin medallions cooked in sauerkraut, and much more.

Accommodations: 51 rooms, 35 with private bath. *Pets:* Permitted in some areas — inquire beforehand. *Driving Instructions:* Minnesota Route 61 and Route 60 go through the town of Wabasha. The inn is on the main street.

Winona, Minnesota

THE HOTEL
129 West Third Street, Winona, MN 55987. 507-452-5460. *Inn-keepers:* Roberta and Michael Taube. Open all year.

Imagine that the year is 1892 and you are one of the Midwest's leading entrepreneurs. On a business trip to Winona you need a place to stay that is fitting for a person of your station. The only logical choice then would be to register at Joseph Schlitz's hotel, just two blocks from the Mississippi, where you could not only enjoy fine lodging but also entertain your business associates in the hotel's famed Sample Room, which offers only the finest wines, liquors, and cigars.

Today the boom times of the Victorian period, when Winona was considered the center of the lumbering industry on the Upper Mississippi, are long gone. But the Schlitz remains—now fully restored and renamed, simply, The Hotel.

The two upper floors of the building contain its guest rooms, their walls done in gentle pastel colors, setting off the floral shades with coordinated drapes at each window. Reproduction Victorian tufted furniture, thick carpets, color television sets, and room telephones are typical of guest accommodations here. Brass or Victorian wooden beds are the rule at the Hotel, and all rooms have been fitted out with modern bathrooms. The restaurant, Yesterdays, offers filet, baby back ribs, and popovers filled with chicken or seafoods. There is a salad bar at dinner and lunch.

Accommodations: 24 rooms with private bath. *Pets:* Discouraged. *Driving Instructions:* Take Route 61 to Winona. The Hotel is at the corner of Third and Johnson streets, downtown.

Ohio

THE BUXTON INN

313 East Broadway, Granville, OH 43023. 614-587-0001. *Innkeepers:* Orville and Audrey Orr. Open all year.

The Buxton Inn has been in continuous operation since it was built in 1812 by Samuel Thrall as the third tavern in the newly settled village. For many years the inn served as the Granville Post Office and a popular stop on the stagecoach line from Newark, Ohio, to Columbus. In the basement, one can still see the large fireplace where the early stage drivers cooked their meals and slept under hand-hewn beams on beds of straw. In 1852 a two-story wing was added to the original building so that the structure formed a U shape with a central courtyard. The property was purchased in 1865 by Major Buxton of Alexandria, and he and his wife operated it as a hotel for forty years, until his death in 1905. The current innkeepers purchased the place in 1972 and spent two years researching and restoring it.

Today, the Buxton Inn is almost as it was a hundred or more years ago. Perhaps one of its most unusual features is that it was constructed almost entirely of black walnut, including much of the frame, the siding, and the pillars. The exterior is painted a peach color selected to reflect its New England heritage. The front portion is the oldest and now contains the gift shop, lobby, and main dining room on the first floor and a two-bedroom suite and two private dining rooms on the second. The 1852 addition to the rear of the inn contains the Victorian dining room on the first floor and two guest rooms on the second. Also upstairs is the original ballroom of the early tavern. It is

used for receptions, special parties, and as an accessory dining room on weekends.

The Buxton Inn serves breakfast to its guests and has full luncheon and dinner menus for guests and the public alike. Several seafood selections include fresh Boston scrod sautéed with lemon butter, brook trout stuffed with mushroom dressing, coquille of seafood cardinale, and a fresh fish of the day. Other choices at dinner include quiche, chicken, sautéed beef liver with tangy orange sauce, several kinds of steak, and prime ribs. Two favorite soups are black mushroom with whipped cream and cream of chicken curry with green grapes and toasted almonds. There is a wide selection of rich desserts and a rather large wine list.

There are three guest rooms in the inn. One is a two-bedroom suite with Eastlake Victorian furnishings that blend with the Oriental rugs covering the hand-pegged walnut plank floors. The first of the upstairs bedrooms in the 1852 wing is done in Empire furnishings that include a large sleigh bed. The other is actually a mini-suite with a very small room with a double bed and a larger room with an assortment of Victorian furniture. The Orrs have also acquired an 1817 building which has 5 additional guest rooms.

The entire inn is centrally air-conditioned in the summer, and there are fireplaces in the lobby and the main dining room for extra comfort in the winter. The Buxton Inn has been placed in the National Register of Historic Places.

Accommodations: 15 rooms with private bath. *Pets:* Not Permitted. *Driving Instructions:* From Columbus take Route 70 to Route 37 and drive north. Granville is 9 miles north of I-70.

THE BEACH HOUSE

213 Kiwanis Avenue, Chaska Beach, Huron, OH 44839. 419-433-5839. *Innkeeper:* Donna J. Lendrum. Open May through October.

The Beach House, which sits on the shore of Lake Erie, with its own private beach just across the lawn, is but a short stroll from the local fishing dock. The inn is of fairly recent vintage and is an assemblage of three barns, antique stained-glass windows, a stone-arched breezeway, and a greenhouse. The guest rooms, in a wing of the house with its own entrance, are furnished in antiques. Innkeeper Donna Lendrum bakes the breakfast treats, which are served with freshly squeezed orange juice or fresh fruit in season. In warm weather, breakfasts are served on the screened porch overlooking the lake. On cooler mornings, everyone gathers around the kitchen table in the warmth from the fire in the kitchen fireplace.

Accommodations: 3 rooms with shared bath. *Pets:* Not permitted. *Children:* Under twelve not permitted. *Driving Instructions:* The inn is two blocks north of U.S. 6 and Route 2 at the eastern edge of Huron, midway between Cleveland and Toledo.

POOR RICHARDS INN

317 Maple, Lakeside, OH 43440. 419-798-5405. *Innkeeper:* Chris Christopher. Open Memorial Day through Labor Day; May and September by reservation.

Lakeside, a summer resort community bordering Lake Erie, is the setting for this informal bed-and-breakfast inn. When the Christophers purchased the building, which had originally opened as a summer hotel in 1885, the townspeople wished them well with the ''poor Richards' house.'' The name appealed to the Christophers so much that they kept it when they reopened the doors. There are numerous touches of humor, such as Ben Franklin's portrait and aphorisms, which are prominently displayed. The inn is decorated in a 1930s style incorporating lots of greenery and wicker furniture, with magazines from the 1940s and 1950s to sustain the mood. Breakfast is the only meal served; however, guests may prepare other meals in the communal kitchen— alcoholic beverages are not permitted. There is a small reading lounge on the second floor, and a large first floor lounge has a number of table games. Poor Richard's is an unpretentious, family-oriented place that vacationers can use as a homebase while exploring the area's attractions.

Accommodations: 33 rooms, 7 with private bath. *Pets:* Not permitted. *Driving Instructions:* From Port Clinton, drive east on Route 163 to Shore Boulevard. Turn north to Gates of Lakeside. Turn left at the first stop sign, Maple street; the inn is in the middle of the second block.

THE GOLDEN LAMB

27 South Broadway, Lebanon, OH 45036. 513-932-5065. *Innkeeper:* Jackson Reynolds. Open daily except Christmas Day.

The Golden Lamb, a large four-story street-front hotel, has been offering overnight accommodations to travelers ever since Jonas Seaman was issued a license to operate a "house of public entertainment" in 1803. Additions to the building occurred in the decades immediately following, and today the inn offers guests a choice of seventeen guest rooms as well as nine dining rooms. The lobby of the hotel sets the stage for the inn as a whole. Many early Ohio antique pieces grace the room, including a fine Regina music box that still plays the old steel-disc records. The lobby has a working fireplace, and the four first-floor dining rooms are entered from the lobby. The dining rooms are filled with antiques, as are many of the hallways throughout the inn. The Shaker Dining Room, for example, has walls lined with pegs on which hang numerous Shaker items, most of which are used daily. The inn prides itself on its collection of Shaker furniture and accessories, largely from the immediate area. In addition to the Shaker collection, the inn displays a large number of Currier and Ives prints on the walls. Guests and day visitors who wish to see more of the inn's Shaker collection are directed to the fourth floor, where two rooms have been established as museum rooms and are glassed in to allow viewing only. In addition to the lobby and dining rooms on the first floor, the Black Horse Tavern, just off the Lebanon Dining Room near the rear of the building, is maintained in mid-nineteenth-century style with a long bar. The walls are decorated with old flintlock rifles and numerous horse-racing items. Horse racing was then and is today an important part of the life in Lebanon.

Each guest room is decorated in a different manner, using Shaker and other antique furniture where possible. The Charles Dickens Room (named for a guest at the inn in 1842) has a replica of the Lincoln bed as its centerpiece. Along with the high-back carved bed are a marble-topped dresser with mirror and several Victorian chairs. The bathroom, like the others in the inn, is of more modern construction. The William McKinley Room, named after one of eleven presidents who have visited the inn, has a canopied four-poster, wing chairs, an antique secretary, and a view over the balcony to Main

Street below. The balcony, a dominant part of the building facade, is a three-story construction but is not accessible from the guest rooms.

The inn features several selections daily at dinner. Turkey in various forms has become one of the favorites. The inn serves fresh turkey raised especially for its kitchen by a local farm. Other menu regulars include roast duck with giblet or orange gravy and a lamb selection, such as roast leg or lamb shanks. There are also daily steak selections. The inn imports fresh trout from Tennessee. A regional favorite is the pan-fried Kentucky (salt-cured) ham steak served with a bourbon glaze. Among the numerous dessert selections are the popular Sister Lizzie's Shaker sugar pie, Harvey Wallbanger cake, and a pecan pie that uses the recipe developed by Abigail Adams.

Accommodations: 19 rooms with private bath. *Pets:* Not permitted. *Driving Instructions:* The inn is in the center of Lebanon, which is most easily reached by taking Route 63 east from I-75 or Route 123 northwest from I-71.

THE BLACKFORK INN

303 North Water Street, Loudonville, Ohio. Mailing address: Box 149, Loudonville, OH 44842. 419-994-3252. *Innkeepers:* Sue and Al Gorisek. Open all year.

The Blackfork Inn was built in 1865 by Philip J. Black, a Civil War merchant who brought the railroad to the village. Listed in the National Register of Historic Places, this fine example of Second Empire architectural styling is being carefully restored with the help of a professional preservationist. All of the inn's rooms are furnished with Ohio antiques augmented by custom-made leather sofas and chairs. Bedrooms generally have heavy brass beds, although one room is furnished with a complete Victorian walnut bedroom suite made in Painesville, Ohio, for Sue Gorisek's great grandmother. A display case in the entrance features Garfield drape-pattern glass produced after the assassination of President Garfield, who preached in the area. Wall plaques in each room describe the significant furnishings and Audubon prints displayed throughout. Bathrooms have oak pull-chain toilets, luxurious linens, hand-milled soaps, and terrycloth robes to pamper guests. Breakfast at the Blackfork is a three-course meal with fresh local fruits and breakfast treats produced by the local Amish community.

Accommodations: 6 rooms with private bath. *Pets and children:* By prior arrangement only. *Driving Instructions:* From I-70, exit on Route 30 east. Then take Route 60 into Loudonville to Main Street; turn north onto North Water Street and continue two blocks to the inn.

Marblehead, Ohio

OLD STONE HOUSE INN

133 Clemons Street, Marblehead, OH 43440. 419-798-5922. *Innkeepers:* Don and Nilene Cranmer. Open all year except December. Old Stone House Inn is at the very tip of Marblehead Peninsula, which juts out into Lake Erie. The 1861 inn, built as a private home by Alexander Clemons, founder of the first local stone quarry, has 128 feet of lake frontage and offers views of Kelley's Island and its ferries. The enclosed widow's walk at the top of the thirty-two-room mansion was used during the Civil War by Union troops as a lookout when rumors spread that an invasion might be launched from Canada across the frozen lake. Today, the innkeepers offer lodging in twelve simply furnished, old-fashioned guest rooms that share six baths on the second and third floors, each with an antique chest of drawers and brass clothes tree. Breakfast is served in the dining room, which has windows overlooking the lake, and the Cranmers run an antique shop in the mansion's former summer kitchen. The peninsula is a resort area with many restaurants and lakeside activities.

Accommodations: 12 rooms with hall baths. *Pets:* Not permitted. *Children:* Under 6 not permitted. *Driving Instructions:* From Port Clinton, take Route 163 east to Marblehead Peninsula and turn left on Clemons Street.

Old Washington, Ohio

ZANE TRACE BED AND BREAKFAST

Main Street, Old Washington, Ohio. Mailing address: P.O. Box 115, Old Washington, OH 43768. 614-489-5970 or 301-757-0929 (off season). *Innkeeper:* Ruth D. Wade. Open May to mid-November.

Old Washington is one mile off I-70 between Wheeling, West Virginia, and Columbus, Ohio. The large, brick Italianate Victorian home was built along the Old National Trail in 1859. It retains its sweeping staircase, 14-foot-high ceilings, arched window casings, and original louvered window shutters. The bedroom fireplaces are closed for insurance purposes, but the fireplace in the breakfast room is lit on chilly mornings. The parlor is furnished with Victorian antiques, and crystal chandeliers appear to be everywhere—even in the main bathroom. The carpeted guest rooms are furnished with an eclectic blend of Victorian bedsteads, bureaus from the thirties, and more modern pieces. Colorful quilts cover the beds. Ruth Wade has added a heated outdoor swimming pool that can be used from early May through Halloween.

Accommodations: 4 rooms with shared baths. *Pets:* Not permitted. *Driving Instructions:* From I-70 take Exit 186 north to Main Street. Turn right. The inn is on the left.

WILLOWTREE INN

1900 West State Route 571, Tipp City, OH 45371. 513-667-2957.
Innkeeper: Martha DeBold. Open all year.

Willowtree Inn, a Federal-style building on several landscaped acres, looks somewhat like a southern mansion transported to the middle of Ohio. The estate was built between 1827 and 1830 by a pioneer Quaker family who re-created their North Carolina home on 1,000 acres of farmland. One wing was added at the end of the Civil War. By the time the DeBolds bought the house, it had stood empty for several years. After months of restoration, the mansion, surrounded by rows of tall shade trees and numerous outbuildings, reopened in a state of renewed elegance. There are four working fireplaces, including one in the dining room, where a Continental breakfast is served. Guest rooms are furnished with a variety of antiques that reflect the several historical periods through which the house has passed. They have plump comforters and extra pillows for reading in bed. Guests are welcome to use the living room, where the only television resides.

Accommodations: 4 rooms, 2 with private bath. *Pets:* Not permitted. *Children:* Under 13 not permitted. *Driving Instructions:* From I-75 north of Dayton, take the Route 571 exit.

Worthington, Ohio

WORTHINGTON INN

649 High Street, Worthington, OH 43085. 614-885-2600. Open all year.

In 1831, R.D. Coles, hearing that a toll road was to be built through Worthington, purchased three lots for $250. As soon as the road was finished, he built a stagecoach stop on his lots. An immediate success, his inn grew steadily over the next century. By 1970, however, the inn had fallen into disrepair. Restored in 1983, it is now a handsome Victorian re-creation complete with Sheraton, Chippendale, and Victorian antique furnishings. The dining rooms, main entry, ballroom, and upper sitting room are original to the inn. Although the guest rooms were constructed during the restoration, they incorporate many elements rescued from other historic buildings: There are wall panels and doors from a county courthouse, plaster ceiling rosettes from the Columbus train station, and a handsome window from an 1822 inn. All the suites have period wallpaper, stenciled walls, and antiques collected from the region.

The restaurant offers a Continental breakfast to guests and lunch and dinner to the public, with an emphasis on American regional dishes. The first floor Pub Room has as its bar an 1880s soda fountain of alabaster, perlatino, mahogany, and stained glass. On the lower level, a wine bar serves vintage wines, champagnes, and hors d'oeuvres.

Accommodations: 26 rooms and suites, all with private bath. *Pets:* Not permitted. *Driving Instructions:* The inn is 8 miles north of Columbus. From I-270, take Route 315 south to Worthington. The inn is at the corner of New England Avenue.

Wisconsin

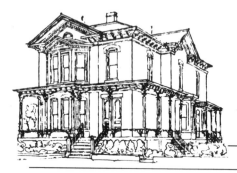

Alma, Wisconsin

LAUE HOUSE

1111 South Main Street, Alma, WI 54610. 608-685-4923. *Innkeepers:* Jerry and Jan Schreiber. Open March through December. Laue House was built in 1863 by a German-born lumber baron who had started the first sawmill in the area a few years earlier. The house, built of locally cast red brick, is a fine example of the Italianate style and is included in the National Register of Historic Places. The owners, Jan and Jerry Schreiber, carefully restored the home using the original plans found in the attic. After talking to a 94-year-old relative of the lumber baron's, they were able to match closely the original wallpaper, carpeting, furniture, and lighting fixtures.

The inn overlooks the Mississippi River, and there is a boat landing just across the scenic Great River Road. The atmosphere at Laue House is friendly and casual. If the Schreibers are out, guests can fill out their own registration ticket, pick a room, and move in. The lobby is set up for get-togethers with a player piano for guests' use. Boats, bikes, and canoes can be rented, and the innkeepers will gladly steer guests to tennis, golf, and their favorite canoeing or picnicking spots.

Accommodations: 7 rooms with shared baths. *Driving Instructions:* The inn is on the Great River Road, Route 35, which becomes Main Street in Alma.

Baraboo, Wisconsin

THE BARRISTER'S HOUSE

226 Ninth Avenue, Box 166, Baraboo, WI 53913. 608-356-3344.
Innkeepers: Glen and Mary Schulz. Open June through August;
weekends only the rest of the year.

When architect Frank Riley designed this green-shuttered, white-brick
house in 1933, he chose the late eighteenth century as his model. The
resulting New England–style home was first occupied by a prominent
Baraboo attorney, thus accounting for its present name. French doors
lead from the large central foyer, while a crystal chandelier and a black
Belgian-marble fireplace provide touches of elegance to the dining
room. Across the foyer is a somewhat less formal living room with
a large white fireplace. A paneled library provides guests with a quiet
place to relax by the fireside.

Each guest room occupies a corner of the house: The Maid's Room,
named for its location at the back of the house, is furnished with 1930s
pieces. The Colonial Room has a view of the city and Baraboo bluffs
and is furnished with reproduction eighteenth-century furniture. The
Barrister's Room has a cherry half-tester bed, and the Garden Room
is furnished with wicker and wrought iron. Weather permitting, guests
may elect to have a Continental breakfast served on the screened porch
or on the terrace.

Accommodations: 4 rooms with private bath. *Pets:* Not permitted. *Children:* Not comfortable for small children. *Driving Instructions:* Route 33 into Baraboo; north onto Birch for 1 block.

GREUNKE'S INN

17 Rittenhouse Avenue, Bayfield, WI 54814. 715-779-5480. *Innkeepers:* Judith Lokken-Strom and Alan Waite. Open April to October.

Stepping into Greunke's Inn is much like stepping into one of Norman Rockwell's *Saturday Evening Post* illustrations. Little has changed here since the late 1940s. The ice cream parlor walls display 1945 Coca-Cola calendars and trays. An old stuffed fish, snagged long ago, guards the archway to the washrooms with their glossy dark-green paint. Guests relax in the lobby to the soulful strains of Hank William's "Your Cheatin' Heart" and Rosemary Clooney's "Hey There" played on the old Wurlitzer jukebox with its tubes of bright colors. This is a gathering spot for lodgers, the scene of many late-night get-togethers.

The inn stands amid birches and maples at one of Bayfield's central intersections. The red wood-frame building with black shutters, built in the 1870s, could easily blend into the main street of any one of Rockwell's New England towns. Innkeepers Judith and Alan have carefully maintained the inn's uncomplicated atmosphere and a look that has remained untouched since the days of ownership by the Greunke family in the late 1940s and the early 1950s.

A small dining room is decorated with 1940s prints, drawings, and antiques. It opens for business at 5 A.M. for local fishermen. Judith

preserves all kinds of berries and fruits and bakes homemade pies, cakes, and pastries. House specialties are the poached whitefish and an unusual dish, whitefish livers. One original Greunke recipe, Trout Hemingway, was written up in *Bon Appetite*. It is fresh lake trout breaded with sesame seeds and cooked in butter with fresh lime and lemon. There are wild-blueberry pancakes and pancakes topped with strawberries and whipped cream. The homemade pea soup is a daily favorite.

The warmth of the inn extends upstairs to the guest rooms, which are completely furnished with antiques of the bygone era. At the top of the stairs is an old working Swedish wall phone that guests love. A small second-floor porch on the east side of the hotel offers guests views of Lake Superior.

Accommodations: 6 rooms sharing hall baths. *Driving Instructions:* Bayfield is on Route 13, at the very top of the state, 70 miles east of Duluth.

OLD RITTENHOUSE INN

301 Rittenhouse Avenue, Bayfield, Wisconsin. Mailing address: Box 584, Bayfield, WI 54814. 715-779-5111. *Innkeepers:* Jerry and Mary Phillips. Open May through October and weekends during the rest of the year.

The Old Rittenhouse Inn is an 1890s mansard-roofed Victorian mansion. The foyer retains its early chair-rail-height cherry paneling, and as you enter the dining rooms, you are struck by the variety of Victorian lighting fixtures that have been restored and are in use. Mary and Jerry Phillips were collectors of period lighting devices before they became innkeepers. They quip that they were forced to buy the inn just to have a place to use all their lamps.

The dining rooms all have working fireplaces and are papered with Victorian prints. The round or square turn-of-the-century oak tables have matching oak chairs. The inn's collection of Victorian hand-embroidered linens is used daily, and there are plants around all of the dining rooms. Service here is formal, in the Victorian tradition, with waiters dressed in ruffled shirts, vests, bow ties, and black trousers, while waitresses wear long Victorian-style dresses with ruffles and long sleeves.

Meals are prepared by Mary Phillips and her staff. The menu, changed weekly, features a choice of six entrées daily. Accompanying the entrée would be the daily breads such as onion dill or orange

walnut. Salad might be wild blackberries and blueberries, strawberries, and bananas in a French cream dressing. The dessert to accompany this meal might be a pot de crème. Reservations are almost always necessary.

Eight rooms have working fireplaces. Several have four-poster beds, while others have king-size brass beds. On the bed are hand-crocheted bedspreads and quilts. Each room has a generous supply of books, one or two rockers, and most, a view of Lake Superior, which is just two blocks away.

Accommodations: 9 rooms, with private bath. *Pets:* Not permitted. *Children:* Not encouraged. *Driving Instructions:* Bayfield is on Route 13, 70 miles east of Duluth.

Cedarburg, Wisconsin

STAGECOACH INN

W61 N520 Washington Avenue, Cedarburg, WI 53012. 414-375-0208 or 375-3035. *Innkeepers:* Brook and Liz Brown. Open all year.

Brook and Liz Brown have breathed new life into the old Stagecoach Inn in Cedarburg. The sturdy stone building has been taking in guests since 1853, when it was built as the Central House Hotel. The Browns' restoration has included stripping more than a century of paint off the building's woodwork, adding border stenciling to the walls, and furnishing with period pieces, including a 100-year-old back bar which graces the pub, where wine, beer, and other beverages are available. Guest rooms have antique furnishings complementing the English country comforters and rag rugs on polished wood floors. Breakfast, the only meal served, includes hot croissants, cereal, juice and coffee. A chocolate shop and bookshop share the first floor with the pub.

Accommodations: 9 rooms, all with private bath. *Pets:* Not permitted. *Smoking:* Not permitted. *Driving instructions:* From Milwaukee, drive north 17 miles on I-43 to exit 17. Take Highway C west 3 miles to Cedarburg. Turn north on Route 57 (Washington Street) to the inn.

WASHINGTON HOUSE INN

W62 N573 Washington Avenue, Cedarburg, WI 53012. 414-375-3550. *Innkeeper:* Judy Drefahl. Open all year.

Cedarburg, about 20 miles north of downtown Milwaukee, is an energetic country town whose history is captured in its many surviving nineteenth-century buildings. The Stone Mill Winery and Cedar Creek Settlement include a functioning winery and about 30 shops and restaurants that have been created from an 1864 stone woolen mill. Just a few blocks from the winery and shops is the Washington House Inn, a restored 1886 brick building. Built as a hotel, it was converted to offices and apartments in the 1920s but was restored to its original purpose during a major renovation in 1983 and 1984. A collection of Victorian furniture and period reproductions were installed in the rooms, which also have televisions, telephones, and radios. Beds are topped with cozy down comforters, and fresh flowers provide color in the guest and public rooms. A social hour takes place each afternoon, and a Continental breakfast of home-baked muffins, cakes, and breads is provided in the morning. To reinforce the air of Victorian authenticity, recipes used in the preparation of the morning breads come from a turn-of-the-century Cedarburg cookbook.

Accommodations: 20 rooms with private bath. *Pets:* Not permitted. *Driving Instructions:* Take I-43 to the Pioneer Road exit (17). Drive west 3 miles to Route 57 and turn right. Drive to the center of town and the inn.

Delavan, Wisconsin

THE ALLYN HOUSE

511 East Walworth Avenue, Delavan, Wisconsin. Mailing address: P.O. Box 429, Delavan, WI 53115. 414-728-9090. *Innkeepers:* Joe Johnson and Ron Markwell. Open all year (Thursday through Sunday off-season).

In the latter half of the nineteenth century, Delavan was the winter home for twenty-six circuses, including P.T. Barnum's, and it was here that the idea for his three-ring circus was born. Almost 150 members of that early circus colony are buried in Delavan. The Allyn House, designed by one of Milwaukee's most prominent architects of the time, Edward Townsend Mix, was constructed in 1885.

Many of the unusual architectural features of this twenty-three-room mansion have been preserved, including the original hand-powered elevator and large Diocletian (horseshoe-shaped) window above the stairway landing. The innkeepers have enhanced the elegance through the use of many formal Victorian pieces in both the guest and common rooms, which augment the stained-, leaded-, cut-, and etched-glass mirrors, windows, and doors. The original inlaid wood floors have been restored, and electrified gasoliers now illuminate the rooms. Guests are welcomed with late afternoon wine and cheese set out in the main parlor, with its hand-painted ceiling and elaborate French Revival parlor set. A full breakfast is served in the sitting room or in the formal, oak-paneled dining room.

Accommodations: 4 rooms with shared bath. *Pets and children:* Not permitted. *Smoking:* Not permitted. *Driving Instructions:* The inn is in the center of Delavan on Route 11 (Walworth Avenue).

Ellison Bay, Wisconsin

THE GRIFFIN INN

11976 Mink River Road, Ellison Bay, WI 54210. 414-854-4306.

Innkeepers: Jim and Laurie Roberts. Open all year.

The Griffin Inn, a gambrel-roofed, shuttered building, was constructed in 1910. Today, it is an inviting New England–style inn in Wisconsin's Door County. The lounge has a stone fireplace and Queen Anne–style furnishings. The spacious dining room has a wood stove. Here hearty country breakfasts are served all year, with lunch and New England–style five-course dinners served during the winter months, when the inn is particularly popular with cross-country skiiers. Guests can come in from a day on the cross-country trails or from skating on the lake to warm themselves before the fire.

The entire inn is filled with artwork, including watercolors by Door County artists. All the guest rooms upstairs are quaintly decorated, many with handmade quilts on antique beds. In addition, there are four cottage units.

The inn has five acres of grounds shaded by maple trees. Fishing, boating, and sandy-beach swimming are within walking distance, and the many other attractions of Wisconsin's Door County are within a short drive. Door County has more miles of shoreline than any other in the nation, as well as the largest inland shipbuilding port.

Accommodations: 10 rooms with shared bath and 4 cottages with private bath. *Pets:* Not permitted. *Children:* Permitted in cottages only. *Driving Instructions:* From Milwaukee, take I-43 north to Manitowoc and Route 42 to Ellison Bay; right on Mink River Road for 2 blocks.

EAGLE HARBOR INN

9914 Water Street, Ephraim, WI 54211. 414-854-2121. *Innkeepers:* Celeste and Richard Wegman. Open all year.

When Celeste and Richard Wegman decided to renovate their white clapboard 1951 house to create a bed-and-breakfast inn, the first thing they did was raise the roof—literally. No sooner was their roof off than a freak blizzard dumped snow on the second-story floors. They quickly closed up the roof, swept aside the snow, and went on to create nine guest rooms with ceiling fans, marble vanities and brass fixtures, and an eclectic collection of antique furnishings gathered from local shops and flea markets. The inn's dining room overlooks spacious wooded grounds. There are pegged floors in the Great Room and the parlor, wallpapers throughout, and fresh flowers and plants. All baked goods are made from scratch, fresh each evening for the next morning's breakfast. In addition to the rooms at the inn, there are twelve cottages, seven of which have housekeeping facilities. The inn is a block from a beach and boat ramp at Green Bay Lake. Charter fishing trips can be arranged on Lake Michigan, and hiking is available at Peninsula State Park, just a mile away.

Accommodations: 9 rooms with private bath and 12 cottages. *Pets and children:* Not permitted. *Driving Instructions:* Take Route 57 north from Green Bay. At Sturgeon Bay, take Route 42 north through northern Door County to Ephraim Bay. The inn will provide detailed driving instructions when reservations are made.

Fish Creek, Wisconsin

WHISTLING SWAN (formerly Proud Mary Inn)

Route 42, Fish Creek, Wisconsin. Mailing address: P.O. Box 193, Fish Creek, WI 54212. 414-868-3442. *Innkeepers:* Andy and Jan Coulson. Open May through October and weekends November through April.

The Whistling Swan has done her fair share of traveling, a bit more than most buildings of her age and size. The inn was built around 1889 in Marinette, across Green Bay from Fish Creek. Ten years later Dr. Herman Welcker bought her and had her transported across the bay. No one around these parts remembers if she floated or skated across the bay, but she made it; for here she stands today. Local historians claim it took six steamboat loads of furnishings to fill her rooms.

The inn, originally the sister hotel of Dr. Welcker's White Gull

Inn just down the street, was operated by the Welcker family until 1940. The inns have now been reunited under the current owners, Andy and Jan Coulson. Many of the original furnishings have been restored and more Victorian pieces added, including wicker chairs and rockers, which line the veranda. On chilly days, there is a fire in the lobby. Dr. Welcker's wife's baby-grand piano stands ready to accommodate musical guests. The Whistling Swan serves breakfast to house guests, and the White Gull's dining room, as well as other restaurants, are within easy walking distance. Boat docks and swimming places are just a block away.

Accommodations: 4 rooms and 3 suites with private bath. *Pets:* Not permitted. *Driving Instructions:* The inn is 22 miles north of Sturgeon Bay on Route 42.

WHITE GULL INN

4225 Main Street, Box 159, Fish Creek, WI 54212. 414-868-3517. *Innkeepers:* Andy and Jan Coulson. Open all year except Thanksgiving and Christmas.

The White Gull Inn, a white clapboard house, looks as if it came off a Vermont mountain and ended up on the shore of Green Bay. According to local historians, the White Gull Inn was brought in one piece to Fish Creek from Marinette, Wisconsin, 18 miles across the bay. This feat was accomplished in the dead of winter with the help of a team of sturdy horses, some huge logs, and a very determined new owner, Dr. Weckler.

The main section was built in 1896; the dining room and kitchen were added in the 1940s and expanded in 1978. The inn has wide second-floor verandas and a ground-floor porch with old deacon's benches, a cider press, and a bulletin board announcing community events and sales. The inn has four small, old-fashioned cottages for families. The furnishings at White Gull are what one would expect to find at a turn-of-the-century country inn; many original pieces are still in residence, along with informal Victorian antiques of the period. The rooms have high ceilings, bare wood floors with scatter rugs, and period print wallpapers. The large lobby has a big fireplace, the focal point of the room. The bedrooms are furnished and decorated with country antiques, including old oak and walnut bureaus and old iron bedsteads painted white.

White Gull Inn is famous for its Door County fish boil, which features fresh lake fish, boiled potatoes, homemade coleslaw, hot breads, and mugs of local or imported beers, topped off with a wedge of home-baked cherry pie. Guests sit on the terrace while the Master Boiler, Russ Ostrand, prepares the dinner over a roaring fire and entertains with his accordion at the same time. The dinner, a Midwestern version of the New England clambake, is served rain or shine on Wednesday, Friday, Saturday, and Sunday evenings in summer and Wednesday and Sunday evenings in winter. Reservations must be made well in advance. On evenings when there is no fish boil, a candlelight dinner is served.

Accommodations: 14 rooms, 9 with private bath. *Pets:* Not permitted. *Driving Instructions:* Take Route 42 from either Manitowoc or Sturgeon Bay to Fish Creek (an unincorporated village). In Fish Creek, turn left at the stop sign at the bottom of the hill and go three blocks.

Lake Geneva, Wisconsin

ELEVEN GABLES INN ON THE LAKE

493 Wrigley Drive, Lake Geneva, WI 53147. 414-248-8393. *Innkeeper:* Audrey Milliette. Open all year.

Eleven Gables Inn is at the edge of Geneva Lake, with shaded grounds that include a private pier and lakefront as well as lawns and a picnic area by the water. The inn was built as a private estate in 1847 and converted to a bed-and-breakfast inn in 1965. Guest rooms and suites, with bookshelves and plush pillows, have canopied four-poster or king-size beds. Most rooms have views of the lake, some have kitchenettes, and several have trundle beds for extra guests. One room is festooned with plants and has Oriental rugs on its oak floors, while another serves as a hostel and has bunks and a private entrance and bath. Coach House is a separate building, originally the estate's ice house, that has a deck overlooking the lake, three bedrooms, a kitchen, and a wood-burning stove. The lake offers swimming, fishing, waterskiing, and boating in summer and ice boating and fishing in winter. Both Nordic and downhill skiing are nearby.

Accommodations: 13 rooms or suites, 8 with private bath. *Driving Instructions:* From Milwaukee, take Route 15 southwest to Elkhorn and then Route 12 to Lake Geneva. The inn is on the southeast shore of the lake.

 Lewis, Wisconsin

SEVEN PINES LODGE AND TROUT PRESERVE

P.O. Box 104, Route 35, Lewis, WI 54851. 715-653-2323. *Innkeepers:* Joan and David Simpson. Open all year.

Seven Pines Lodge, a national historic site, is an idyllic country retreat. It was built in 1903 as a private estate by Charles Lewis, a prominent financier. The hand-hewn–log buildings are surrounded by acres of virgin white pine. The parklike grounds immediately around the lodge are reminiscent of a German forest: manicured and tidy with lawns sweeping down to a trout stream. The lodge, constructed by Norwegian craftsmen imported by Mr. Lewis, has exterior walls of logs; but this is no ordinary log cabin. It is the luxuriously appointed, year-round estate of a wealthy man who wanted a secluded haven for his family and friends. Mr. Lewis's guests were famous and powerful people, including presidents and foreign diplomats. The lodge was sold as a private club, and the Simpsons still run it that way. Guests have the option of becoming members, entitling them and their friends to unlimited use of lodge facilities.

Calvin Coolidge enjoyed staying at the lodge. His presidential suite is Seven Pines's most impressive bedroom, with original décor and French doors opening to the sounds of the whispering pines and the nearby stream. The lodge itself retains all the elegantly rustic furnishings of Mr. Lewis's time. The east porch, overlooking the stream and lawns, still is decked out with Victorian-looking ferns and antique wicker with old-fashioned floral cushions. Time appears to have stopped in the early 1900s. The living room and dining room appear to be untouched. Teddy Roosevelt would feel right at home. There are comfortable-looking upholstered chairs and couches, mission furniture, and other oak pieces. A moosehead surveys the room from the wall above the wide brick fireplace, where fires are always burning when it's chilly. The many mementoes, Oriental rugs, and fringed lampshades harken back to a more easygoing life-style.

Guests have the choice of lodgings in one of three log structures on the grounds. The lodge has five rooms, including the presidential suite, several twin-bedded rooms sharing a large common bath, and a loft with four single beds. The Gate House, once Mr. Lewis's private office, is now a guesthouse surrounded by 100-foot-high pines. It has a working fireplace and four beds and a bath. All rooms are decorated with Mr. Lewis's mementoes. The Stream House is quite an experience. It is across a footbridge and looks for all the world like a log mushroom.

Seven Pines offers recreational activities all year. There are 1,000 acres for secluded hikes and cross-country skiing. The stream is stocked with rainbow and brook trout from the breeding pond, and the surrounding area has hundreds of lakes for boating and fishing.

The lodge's dining room is open to guests for all meals and to the public for lunch and dinner by reservation only. The house specialty is the freshly caught trout. Guests wishing to enjoy their own day's catch can do so in style. The kitchen will prepare it any way one wishes.

Accommodations: 7 rooms, 3 with private bath. *Driving Instructions:* The lodge is 1 mile east of Lewis, which is equidistant from Siren and Frederic on Route 35.

Mineral Point, Wisconsin

DUKE HOUSE

618 Maiden Street, Mineral Point, WI 53565. 608-987-2821. *Innkeepers:* Thomas and Darlene Duke. Open all year.

Mineral Point is Wisconsin's third oldest community, founded during the 1830s by adventurous Cornish lead miners who later joined the 49ers and headed west — though not before making their mark on the town with their stone houses and Cornish pastries.

The Duke House was built in 1890 after the miners had departed. Darlene and Tom Duke moved here from Illinois and transformed the house into a bed-and-breakfast inn. Their common room is the setting for before-dinner gatherings, during which guests and innkeepers get acquainted over wine, iced tea, and hors d'oeuvres. There are more opportunities for conversation at breakfast in the dining room. The Dukes prepare pastries, tea biscuits, and scones to serve with the coffee, juice, and teas.

Each of the three guest rooms is unique, with wing chairs, tie backs, and antique beds — one an 1860 spool bed, another a queen-size, lace-canopied four-poster, and still another a pencil-point four-poster.

Accommodations: 3 rooms with shared baths. *Pets and children:* Not permitted. *Driving Instructions:* Mineral Point is on Route 151 between Madison, Wisconsin, and Dubuque, Iowa.

THE WILSON HOUSE INN

110 Dodge Street, Mineral Point, WI 53565. 608-987-3600. *Innkeepers:* Glen and Harriet Ridnour. Open all year.

In the early 1800s, prospectors rushed to Mineral Point in search of the area's large deposits of lead ore. Many came from Cornwall, England, and used their hard-rock mining skills to build homes that survive today as one of the finest collections of stone buildings in the country.

Wilson House is a large Federal-style brick mansion built in the mid-nineteenth century, now decorated with antique country furniture and many quilts.

Guest rooms, decorated with quilts and a variety of Victorian pieces, include one sunny corner room with a high-back Victorian double bed; another has window seats overlooking the yard, a love seat, and a queen-size cannonball bed. A breakfast of fresh fruits and home-baked breads is served in the country kitchen, warmed by an antique Home Comfort wood-burning cookstove.

Accommodations: 4 rooms, 2 with private bath. *Pets:* Permitted only with security deposit. *Driving Instructions:* The inn is on Route 151.

Oshkosh, Wisconsin

MARYBROOKE INN

705 West New York Avenue, Oshkosh, WI 54901. 414-426-4761.
Innkeepers: Mary and Brook Rolston. Open all year.

As a lumber center at the turn of the century, Oshkosh provided much of the oak used in the homes around the area, including Marybrooke, an 1895 home turned inn. The Rolstons get acquainted with guests in the parlor over afternoon tea and sherry. The inn is furnished with many family antiques. Walls are decorated with the Rolstons' collection of prints. A sitting room with a piano attracts guests in the evening. In the morning, a full country breakfast is served in the dining room, but guests may have coffee and muffins served in their rooms.

Accommodations: 4 rooms with shared baths. *Pets and smoking:* Not permitted. *Children:* Under 12 not permitted. *Driving Instructions:* From U.S. 41, exit east on Route 21 and cross the Fox River Bridge to High Avenue. Turn right, then left at New York Avenue.

Poynette is in the southern part of the state, about a half-hour's drive north of Madison. The town of 1,100 is about 6 miles from *Lake Wisconsin*, an enlargement of the Wisconsin River. The lake offers boating, some swimming, fishing, and other water sports. Just outside the village of Poynette is the state-run *Mackenzie Environmental Center*, which includes several well-established nature areas, a state game farm that raises thousands of pheasants annually, and an arboretum.

JAMIESON HOUSE

407 North Franklin Avenue, Poynette, WI 53955. 608-635-4100. *Innkeepers:* Carole and Jim Gacek. Open all year except Christmas. Dining by reservation.

Jamieson house consists of three historic buildings: an early schoolhouse, the 1878 brick home of Hugh Jamieson, and the 1883 brick home of his son, Hugh Pierce Jamieson, across the street. The father's house was carefully restored to its Victorian splendor, employing only true restoration techniques—such as plastering where others might let sheet rock suffice—and repairing the ornamental plaster moldings. The result is a house with three intimate dining rooms on the first floor and two guest suites on the second.

Diners enter the Jamieson House through a reception room that once served as Hugh Jamieson's private office. Coats are hung in the former vault room just off the old office. The room harks to an earlier day when there were no banks in Poynette. The Gold Dining Room, the largest of the three, has an unusual Chickering Square grand piano. The room, named for its gold wallpapers, has four tables surrounded by Hitchcock chairs. The Cranberry Room, adjacent, has an extensive collection of early Cranberry glass, displayed in a corner cupboard, and two polished walnut tables. The third dining room, the Green room, was originally the parlor.

The guest house across the street contains two-room suites and double rooms. Each is provided with carefully selected Victorian antiques in elegant settings. Perhaps the most lavish is the Master Suite, which has reproduction Victorian blue and green wall coverings, a high-backed rare walnut bed, a marble-topped dresser, and, in the full bath-

room, a six-foot sunken tub surrounded by mirrors. The adjacent sitting room has a velvet antique chaise. The Parlour Suite is done in greens and whites and is noted for its east-facing bay window and a bath surrounded by Spanish tiles. In all, the rooms are a perfect complement to the setting at the restaurant. They have no television and no telephone, but all are fully carpeted except the somewhat less formal Sun Room Suite, which retains its hardwood floors. The School House has two suites, each with a hot tub.

Accommodations: 10 rooms with private bath. *Driving Instructions:* Poynette is about 25 miles north of Madison. Take Routes I-90 and 94 north to Route CS, which becomes Main Street in Poynette. Go north on Main Street till you see the inn on your right.

Sturgeon Bay, Wisconsin

BAY SHORE INN
4205 Bay Shore Drive, Sturgeon Bay, WI 54235. 414-743-4551.
Innkeeper: Betty Hanson. Open May through October.

The Bay Shore Inn is a resort on the bay in scenic Door County, Wisconsin. It contains just about every conceivable type of accommodation, but the emphasis is on more contemporary lodging in A-frame or beachfront cottages of recent vintage. The inn has grown up out of an old orchard farm. In 1922 the barn that served the apple industry on the farm was converted into what is now the main lodge. The dining room there still retains the original hardwood floor from its apple storage days. The lodge has an early American atmosphere, with a fireplace in the lobby, couches, rockers, and books scattered about in a homey fashion. Upstairs in the lodge are nine old-fashioned guest rooms.

Also appealing for their historic atmosphere are the Farmhouse rooms. The Farmhouse, built in 1880, is a small and cheerful one-and-a-half–story cottage with a recently added kitchen wing. Much of the original furniture from the last century remains in the three guest rooms (two are suites) available here. The remaining lodgings are offered in the screened-porched Beach Terrace cabins, the Ranch Terraces that face the orchard, six A-frame Chalet cottages, and a two-bedroom cottage called Woodside. All the cabins have contemporary furnishings; most have views of the bay.

The Bayshore was originally developed by John and Matilda Hanson, immigrants from Sweden. The inn's early fame came from the Swedish recipes used by Matilda in her kitchen, many of which are still used by the Hanson children, who currently run the inn. The inn maintains its own garden, which supplies many of its vegetables during the summer season. Breakfasts at the Bay Shore Inn offer not only the expected cereals and eggs but also special Swedish pancakes served with a dish of lingonberries. The breads served at breakfast and throughout the day are all homemade, as are the jellies and jams. At dinner the inn offers four regular items, including steak, ground sirloin, broiled fillet of Lake Michigan whitefish, and a chef's salad. Each day there is a daily special, which may be prime ribs, pork chops, roast chicken or lamb, steak kabobs, or barbecued ribs. Soup is served daily, and a particular house specialty is the cheese soup. On Tuesdays and Fridays the inn offers a Door County fish boil, consisting of boiled fish and potatoes, salad, relish tray, breads, and doughnuts. The fish boil is served in the early evening on the beach.

Recreational facilities at the Bay Shore Inn include a game room in the lodge and a larger separate recreation hall by the beach that offers table tennis, pool, fooz ball, pinball, card tables, and a jukebox. The main focus of attention is on the bay, with swimming, sailing, water skiing, and fishing available at the beachfront. There is a screened outdoor tennis court for guests.

Accommodations: 30 rooms with private bath. *Pets:* Not permitted. *Driving Instructions:* Enter Sturgeon Bay on Business Route 42-57 and cross the bridge. Immediately turn left onto First Avenue. Follow First past the shipyards to the intersection of Iowa and Third Avenue. Turn left on Third (also called Bay Shore Drive and County Road B). The inn is 3 miles from the city at 4205 Bay Shore Drive.

WHITE LACE INN

16 North Fifth Avenue, Sturgeon Bay, WI 54235. 414-743-1105.
Innkeepers: Bonnie and Dennis Statz. Open all year.

The White Lace Inn is comprised of three elegantly restored Victorian houses, one a Queen Anne–style built in 1903; another, an 1880s guest cottage; and the third, an 1898 Victorian on adjoining grounds. All are meticulously restored and feature Victorian antiques and woodwork nicely set off by the yards of lace and antique linens that give the inn its name. The inn is just a few blocks from restaurants, little shops, museums, and a dock for Sturgeon Bay boat tours and charters. After a day of exploring the area or, in winter, a day of cross-country skiing, skating, and tobogganing, the White Lace Inn is a perfect spot to return to. One can curl up in the warmth of the parlor's hearth or work on a jigsaw puzzle set out on one of the antique tables. In summer, guests can enjoy iced tea on the columned front porch.

Rooms throughout are furnished with Victorian antiques, including canopied beds, a big brass bed, and ornate, hardwood beds. Many rooms have working fireplaces. One room has white lace and white wicker, with a canopied brass bed and a small adjoining tower room. Another is decorated in lavenders and forest greens and has an ornate Victorian bed. A third is done in a more formal Victorian style, with an 1840s high-back walnut bed and white and peach decor. Several rooms have double whirlpool baths. A Continental breakfast is served by the sitting-room fireplace or in the oak-paneled dining room.

Accommodations: 15 rooms with private bath. *Pets:* Not permitted. *Children:* Under 12 not permitted. *Driving Instructions:* Take Business 42-57 into Sturgeon Bay and cross the bridge into downtown. You'll be on Michigan Street. Turn left onto Fifth Avenue. The White Lace Inn will be on your right.

White Lake, Wisconsin

WOLF RIVER LODGE

    Langlade, Wisconsin. Mailing address: Post Office, White Lake, WI 54491. 715-882-2182. *Innkeeper:* George Steed. Open April through September and Christmas to mid-March.

White Lake is in northeastern Wisconsin, near the southwestern corner of the Nicolet National Forest. Many visitors to this scenic region come to try their hand at river rafting and fly-fishing on the Wolf River. Each day all summer long, especially on weekends, rafters and canoers take trips down the Wolf ranging in length from 3 to 25 miles. The longer trips start from the north in Lily and end at the border of the Menominee Indian Reservation.

    The lodge is one of four major raft-rental centers and, more importantly, a comfortable log-and-shingle building offering overnight lodging in antique-filled guest rooms. Quilts, samplers, and braided rugs add warmth to the rooms, which tend to be rather small and have a decided rustic flavor, appropriate to the lodge's riverbank setting.

    Breakfasts at the Wolf River Lodge are designed to provide rafters with plenty of stamina for the day ahead and include eggs, jam-filled crepes, sausage or bacon, toast, and coffee. Innkeeper George Steed takes particular pride in the trout served at his lodge. He also offers steaks and duckling. The Nicolet National Forest has miles of hiking and bicycling trails and, in winter, cross-country skiing. The Wolf River Lodge also runs a school for white-water canoeing.

    Accommodations: 8 rooms with shared baths. *Pets:* Not permitted. *Driving Instructions:* Langlade is at the intersection of Routes 55 and 64. Just past the intersection, going north on Route 55, look for the sign for the Wolf River Lodge.

Reminder: Rates and credit-card information are listed in the index.

The Central States

Iowa

VICTORIAN BED AND BREAKFAST INN
425 Walnut Street, Avoca, Iowa. Mailing address: P.O. Box 249, Avoca, IA 51521. 712-343-6336. *Innkeepers:* Andrea and Rodney Murray. Open all year except January to mid-February.

Thomas Moore's Irish melody "The Meeting of the Waters" provided the name of this peaceful southwestern Iowa town, a farming community. The 1904 Victorian, constructed by one of Avoca's leading turn-of-the century contractors, Fred Thielsen, was his own home, which may account for the careful detailing evident throughout. Noteworthy are the fishtail shingling of the exterior and the golden pine woodwork within.

The five guest rooms are furnished with midwestern antiques and have area rugs, hand-sewn quilts and pillows, lace curtains, and wallpapers. The Wild Rose Room is a favorite with honeymooners and includes a sitting area with a marble-topped table and ice cream chairs, a walnut chest and armoire, and a queen-size iron-and-brass bed. Both the dining room, where breakfast is served, and the parlor have detailed columns, large windows, and antique oak furnishings. Andrea, with advance notice, will prepare luncheon and dinner for guests and the public, either from a sample menu or from a menu of their own choosing.

Accommodations: 5 rooms with shared baths. *Pets:* Not permitted. *Children:* Under 13 not permitted. *Smoking:* Not permitted. *Driving Instructions:* From I-80, take exit 40. The inn is 1 mile south on Route 59.

Brooklyn, Iowa

HOTEL BROOKLYN

154 Front Street, Brooklyn, IA 52211. 515-522-9229. *Innkeeper:* Kay Lawson. Open all year.

Set against the Hotel Brooklyn's red-brick face, the curved white lintels over each of its windows make the hotel look rather as if it has raised its eyebrows to peer out at the world going by. Built in 1875, the hotel is noted for its three-story tower, its buttressed gables, and the four Doric columns that support its pediment and porch. Listed in the National Register of Historic Places, the hotel is only a short drive from the Amana Colonies, where travelers may sample German-style cooking and visit the furniture factory, woolen mills, winery, meat markets, and bakeries, as well as the Amana refrigerator factory.

The Hotel Brooklyn's sitting room has a Carrara-marble fireplace and antique mahogany, oaken, and walnut furniture. Guest rooms have king- or queen-size beds, ceiling fans, air conditioning, and TV.

Accommodations: 9 rooms, 3 with private bath. *Pets:* Not permitted. *Driving Instructions:* The inn is halfway between Des Moines and Iowa City on I-80.

Dubuque, Iowa

THE REDSTONE INN

504 Bluff, Dubuque, IA 52001. 319-582-1894. *Innkeeper:* Gail Naughton. Open all year.

A.A. Cooper built this mansion in 1894 as a wedding gift for his daughter. He had made his fortune as a manufacturer of buggies and prairie schooner wagons. As legend has it, A.A. made one tactical error. When approached by young entrepreneur Henry Ford about producing horseless carriages, Cooper turned him down.

In a spare-no-expense restoration, a group of Dubuque business-people rescued the historic mansion and transformed it into an elegant small hotel where guests choose their favorite rooms from the photo book at the oak-paneled reception desk. The parlor features a plaster frieze of gilded cherubs, ribbons, and garlands and bird's-eye maple woodwork, and stained-glass doors and windows illuminate the color scheme used throughout: Mauves, burgundies, deep blues, and greens. The hotel is furnished with high-style Victorian antiques, augmented by luxurious modern bathrooms, including some with whirlpool baths. Guests are served light breakfasts and afternoon tea at a small additional charge.

Accommodations: 15 rooms with private bath. *Pets:* Not permitted. *Driving Instructions:* In Dubuque, take Locust St. north to Fifth St. and turn left. At Bluff, turn west onto Bluff.

Elk Horn, Iowa

THE TRAVELLING COMPANION

4314 Main Street, Elk Horn, IA 51531. 712-764-8932. *Innkeeper:* Karolyn Ortgies. Open all year.

Elk Horn is a quiet little town in the heart of America's largest Danish settlement, where a working windmill, brought over from Denmark, is one of the town's major attractions and where a national Danish heritage museum is planned for construction. As a tribute to Denmark and one of its most beloved citizens—Hans Christian Anderson—Karolyn Ortgies has created an inviting bed-and-breakfast inn. Its name, Travelling Companion, comes from one of Anderson's fairy tales, as do the names of the three guest rooms: The Ugly Duckling, with its swan motif; Little Mermaid, with antiques and soft roses and burgundies; and Thumbelina, furnished with pressed oak and antique toys. Breakfast, served in the guests' rooms, features freshly baked quiches or, most appropriately, Danish pastries.

The 1909 house has as its centerpiece an open staircase with ornate columns of natural, unpainted woods. The sitting room is available for guests' use.

Accommodations: 3 rooms with shared baths. *Pets:* Not permitted. *Driving Instructions:* Take exit 54 north off I-80 and continue 7 miles.

Homestead, Iowa

Early in the eighteenth century a group of inspirationists (German Lutheran separatists) immigrated to this country and eventually settled on thousands of acres of Iowa farmland. They founded seven communal villages known as the Amana Colonies, which are going strong today, although most of the community property has been redistributed as stock and the villagers own their own homes. Farming is still the main industry, but Amana is famous nationwide for a number of products, primarily Amana refrigerators and ranges. Quality of workmanship has made Amana baked goods, hand-crafted furniture, and clocks much sought after. Most of their bakeries, wineries, clock and furniture factories, craft shops, and more are open for public tours. The village of Amana, the society's main headquarters, features butcher shops, a woolen mill and sales outlet, and other tourist attractions. The *Heritage House* in Amana provides visitors with exhibits and audio-visual descriptions of the history of the people and the colonies. Most of the towns have general stores. Middle Amana has a restored kitchen and the *Lily Lake* Homestead, on Route 151, features German restaurants and *Amana Heim*, an early home furnished as it was more than a century ago. It is open to the public April through November.

DIE HEIMAT COUNTRY INN

Amana Colonies, Homestead, IA 52236. 319-622-3937. *Innkeepers:* Don and Sheila Janda. Open all year.

Die Heimat (German for "the home place"), a restored building that has been caring for travelers since 1854, is in Homestead, one of the seven villages that make up the historic Amana Colonies of Iowa. Each village had a communal kitchen providing meals for the villagers, but in 1932 the colonies gave up their communal way of life during the Great Change, and the kitchens were closed. Die Heimat was the kitchen house of Homestead; when that operation closed it became a private home that provided lodging for overnight guests and boarders. In the 1960s it was bought by two enterprising Amana men who gutted the old building and redesigned the interior to include a lounge and guest rooms with private baths. The guest rooms' beds, chairs, sofas, and accessory furniture are manufactured in the colonies at the Amana Furniture Shops. Three large guest rooms feature air conditioning, a wet bar, and refrigerator. The lobby and guest rooms are decorated with art by local Amana people, some family heirlooms, and German "house blessings." The lounge is furnished with such attractive Amana pieces as upholstered rockers and love seats. A social time is at the breakfast table over hot coffee and rolls, toast, and juice. This Continental breakfast is the only meal offered at Die Heimat, but innkeepers Don and Sheila Janda will gladly steer guests to the nearby restaurants featuring Amana's famous German dishes.

Accommodations: 19 rooms with private bath. *Pets:* Not permitted. *Driving Instructions:* Take either Route 151 south from Cedar Rapids or Route 6 west of Iowa City to Homestead. The inn is on Main Street.

Mount Pleasant, Iowa

This is the home of historic *Iowa Wesleyan University*, founded in the mid-nineteenth century by the Methodist Church and John Harlan, president of the Mount Pleasant Collegiate Institute, which formed the nucleus for the university. In 1855, Harlan became a Republican U.S. senator from Iowa and held that office throughout the Civil War years. He was Abraham Lincoln's close personal friend and served as secretary of the interior under Andrew Johnson after Lincoln's assassination. In 1868, Harlan's daughter Mary married Lincoln's eldest son, Robert Todd Lincoln.

HISTORIC HARLAN HOUSE

122 North Jefferson Street, Mount Pleasant, IA 52641. 319-385-3126. *Innkeeper:* Michael Richards. Open all year.

The 1857 portion of the Harlan Hotel is sandwiched between two sections that were added at the turn of the century when the original residence was converted to a hotel. The hotel is an ivy-covered brick building with white wood trim and a pillared entrance. The ivy almost completely hides the brick and even reaches over some of the windows. This is an old-fashioned Midwestern small-town establishment in the best tradition. The middle section of the hotel was once the home of Senator John Harlan, a close friend of Lincoln's and father-in-law to Lincoln's eldest son. The young Lincolns inherited the house and later sold it to be a hotel. The original part of the house contains a dining room used for private parties. This Lincoln-Harlan Room has been restored and contains a working fireplace, period furnishings, and many interesting mementos of the hotel's early days.

The large lobby contains desks, lounging chairs, and a big fireplace where fires are lit on chilly days and nights. The centerpiece of the room is an old Regulator grandfather's clock. The lobby also has a travel agency and a gift shop. Off the lobby are the only ground-floor guest quarters, a spacious suite of rooms with a private bath. The second and third floors contain the rest of the guest rooms. The inn-keeper has begun a long-range program for the upstairs guest rooms, restoring the entire hotel to its early Victorian-era elegance.

The dining room downstairs offers Iowa dishes to travelers, guests, and townspeople every day but Sunday. The menu changes daily and features a wide variety of "down home" cooking with platters of roast beef, pork, beef stews, beef and noodle casseroles, meatloaf, hamloaf, pork chops, and—every Friday—fish. The house favorite is the big bowl of homemade soup. The other "constant" is lemon pie every Saturday; for more than thirty years people have flocked here on Saturdays to have a slice or two or three of the Harlan House lemon pie.

Accommodations: 38 rooms, 14 with private bath, and a suite. *Driving Instructions:* The hotel is 27 miles west of Burlington (on the Mississippi River) on Route 34 in the heart of Mount Pleasant at the intersection with Route 218, which links Minneapolis and St. Louis. Mount Pleasant is the midpoint.

Stone City, Iowa

THE INN AT STONE CITY

Stone City, Iowa. Mailing address: R.R. 1, Stone City, IA 52205. 319-385-3126. *Innkeepers:* Michael and Lynette Richards. Open all year.

The Ronen family came from Ireland in the late nineteenth century, opened a stone quarry, and in 1903 built themselves a fine mansion of stone on a hilltop overlooking the beautiful Wapsipinicon River Valley. In the 1930s the famous painter Grant Wood founded a highly respected art colony in Stone City, and the estate was used to house the women members of the colony. Today the estate is an inn—a restful sanctuary for artists, writers, and seekers of tranquility. The Inn at Stone City, coed now, stands on 25 acres of rolling lands. The fields and woods are home to many a wild turkey and deer, as well as a profusion of wildflowers and mushrooms. In the spring the highly prized morel mushrooms are harvested and served at the inn.

This small inn prides itself on its personal service. The guest rooms have been named after artists and writers associated with Grant Wood's colony. Each room is furnished with its own special antiques. The Richardses are quite certain that a muse dwells in the Iowa writer's room. There is almost always a fire in one of the three hearths at the inn.

Leisurely meals are served family style around a large "thresher's" table. It is a fine place to get acquainted with fellow lodgers and visitors. The inn offers three meals a day to guests and the public alike. Two of the specialties of the house are the seasoned rolled roast and "Gramma's" chicken and biscuits.

The Richardses also own the Stone City General Store nearby. Built in the 1890s, it was in operation until 1971. It now houses a dining room and Stonecutters Pub, with a large stone hearth and lots of singing and conversation. Many consider the pub the center of acoustic and folk music in Iowa.

In summer the most popular sport here is canoeing down the Wapsipinicon and Buffalo rivers. Canoe rentals are available. In winter there is cross-country skiing, with rentals and instruction available. Many visitors feel there is an unusual therapeutic quality about the area and the inn and make annual "self-healing" retreats here. The Richardses assist people by recommending a variety of skilled practitioners of natural healing arts on request.

Accommodations: 7 rooms with shared baths. *Driving Instructions:* Take Route 1 north from I-80 to Anamosa, then drive 3 miles west to Stone City.

Kansas

HARDESTY HOUSE

    712 Main Street, Ashland, KS 67831. 316-635-2911. *Innkeeper:* Kevin Brown. Open all year.

Hardesty House is a two-story brick, tile, and concrete hotel dating back to the early 1900s. The hotel welcomes guests today with room after room of turn-of-the-century furnishings. When you enter the lobby, you see a wide stairway to the second floor. A cashier's cage from an early bank, old rockers, benches, and a hat tree establish the period flavor. Hanging from the lobby walls are pictures of people and events from the Ashland area's past, as well as kerosene lamps with metal reflectors. There is an ornate old heating stove that still functions, although it has been converted to gas for convenience. The old-fashioned wallpaper and the pressed-tin ceilings, complete with metal faces in the corners, reinforce the feeling of yesteryear.

    The Hardesty House Hotel has recently added the Second Century restaurant and club. The dining room displays old farm implements, a bearskin rug, a moose head, and more pictures of the Ashland area. Old-fashioned dolls and kerosene lamps stand on top an old piano; antique chairs surround round oak tables. Dinners include smoked

meats, seafood, and steaks, with nightly specials that include Chinese or Mexican dishes, calf fries, shrimp peel, and an all-you-can-eat Sunday buffet. The dining room is closed on Mondays.

Off the lobby is a sitting room with a hanging stained-glass lamp, a Victorian velvet love seat, several rockers, an oak bookcase-and-desk combination, a small "oak heater," a bentwood easel, a magazine rack, more old pictures, and a marble-topped occasional table.

Several guest rooms are furnished with brass beds, and one has an early walnut-backed bed. Each has chairs, rockers, and dressers, some marble-topped. The walls are covered with reproduction early American papers, and the baths have either old wooden or other antique mirrors and light fixtures. In addition to regular rooms, there are two apartments. One is a studio room with some antique furnishings; the other has one bedroom, a living room, a kitchen, and a bathroom. Both have air conditioning.

Accommodations: 12 rooms with private bath. *Pets:* Not permitted. *Driving Instructions:* The hotel is in Ashland on I-160, approximately 50 miles southeast of Dodge City, Kansas.

Missouri

BORGMAN'S BED AND BREAKFAST

Arrow Rock, MO 65320. 816-837-3350. *Innkeepers:* Kathy and Helen Borgman. Open all year.

Arrow Rock, on the Missouri River, is a national historical landmark. The village marked the beginning of the Santa Fe Trail, the last outpost of civilization before the wagons rolled westward. In the 1850s the town grew to 1,000 people. Today it is a peaceful little river village of 82, with antique and craft shops as well as a repertory theater.

The Borgmans' house was built in 1855 in a classically simple style, with a two-story veranda and white clapboard siding. The wood floors and hand stenciling on the borders of some rooms are set off by colorful handmade rag rugs, quilts, and a comfortable mixture of antiques and newer furnishings. The sitting room has an old windup Victrola, lots of puzzles and games, and a library. The family-style breakfast, served in the kitchen, usually includes one or more of Helen's home-baked breads. Guests frequently find Helen in her kitchen preparing batches of sugar cookies or divinity. There is a daily walking tour of Arrow Rock, which has many restored frontier buildings.

Accommodations: 4 rooms with shared baths. *Pets:* Not permitted. *Driving Instructions:* The inn is 15 miles northwest of Boonville, Missouri, on Route 41.

Hermann, Missouri

BIRK'S GOETHE STREET GASTHAUS

700 Goethe Street, Hermann, MO 65041. 314-486-2911 or 314-486-2973. *Innkeepers:* Elmer and Gloria Birk. Open all year except Thanksgiving and Christmas to New Years.

The innkeepers of this large Gothic Victorian mansion plan special adventure weekends for their guests. The mystery weekends, for example, are complete with visiting psychics, mystery writers, or real-life detectives. Treasure hunts, bed-and-breakfast seminars, and international cooking weekends are offered.

The inn, built in 1866 by one of the owners of the nearby historic Stone Hill Winery, looks as if it were transported from a Charles Addams or Edward Gorey cartoon. The Birks' Victorian furnishings help create the proper period atmosphere: The guest rooms have dust ruffles and warm quilts, while several bathrooms have cast-iron eagle-claw tubs with their talons painted gold. Full breakfasts are served in the dining room, where guests can plan exploration of Hermann, a village rich in German traditions.

Accommodations: 9 rooms, 7 with private bath. *Pets:* Not permitted *Children:* Not permitted. *Driving Instructions:* From I-70, take Route 19 twelve miles south to Hermann. From 6th Street, go west 3 blocks and turn south on Goethe 1 block.

Sainte Genevieve, Missouri

THE INN ST. GEMME BEAUVAIS

78 North Main Street, Sainte Genevieve, Missouri. Mailing address: P.O. Box 231, Sainte Genevieve, MO 63670. 314-883-5744.
Innkeepers: Mr. and Mrs. Norbert Donze. Open all year.

In the late 1840s, Felix Rozier bought property on North Main Street from the Le Clere family and set about building a home designed to withstand the elements for many centuries. The three-story building is made of solid brick, and even the interior walls are 18 inches thick. An early member of the Le Clere family had married the daughter of one Vital St. Gemme Beauvais, and the association between the owners of the property on which the inn now stands and the St. Gemme Beauvais family gave the current innkeepers their name for the inn.

As you step across the broad veranda, its roof supported by six tall columns, you enter the front hall of the inn and immediately face an open staircase leading to the guest rooms above. Hanging in the hall and setting the antique feeling of this restored early building is a four-armed chandelier bearing amber glass shades. The lighting fixture is one of many treasured local antiques collected by the current owners for installation in their inn. It is dated 1849 and was rescued by a local dealer and sold to them. An oak coat tree stands in the hall, and on the floor is ruby-red-and-gold woollen carpeting, complemented by wallpaper that has almost a matching print. Just off the hall is the office papered with traditional pineapple print denoting hospitality. The registration desk is a rolltop type with an old-fashioned spool cabinet on top and a set of post office boxes rescued from an old country store at its side.

The dining room has white walls, and a white marble mantel frames the working fireplace. In the center of the room is a large antique oval table around which are arranged ladderback chairs. In the morning guests assemble here and are served family-style at this or another table. Each day a full breakfast—included in the price of the room —features a great variety of main dishes, among them filled crepes, herb omelets, French toast, and eggs Benedict. For lunch a single entrée is served each day. Among the regulars are quiche Lorraine, chicken-filled crepes, and chicken à la king. The luncheon includes tossed green salad, vegetable, French bread, and dessert. Several

desserts are made but Mrs. Donze is particularly proud of the sherried peach trifle. No dinner is served at the inn, but local restaurants are handy.

Most of the rooms at the inn are private suites of two rooms each, and most are on the second floor, the exceptions being two suites on the ground level and two large rooms on the third floor. The rooms are all decorated with Victorian furniture. Several have coordinated bedroom sets, such as the elaborate mahogany furniture in one room or the oak and walnut sets in two others. Still other rooms have a mixture of woods, but the selection is almost completely Victorian. Half a block from the inn the family has purchased and restored a home, dating from 1770, that has additional guest rooms on the second floor for use when the main inn is full.

Accommodations: 2 rooms and 6 suites, all with private bath. *Pets:* Not permitted. *Driving Instructions:* From Saint Louis travel south on I-55 to Route 32. Exit east on 32 to Route 61. Take 61 to the Sainte Genevieve exit and into town. The inn is on Main Street.

Washington, Missouri

SCHWEGMANN HOUSE

438 West Front Street, Washington, MO 63090. 314-239-5025.
Open all year.

John Schwegmann came to this bustling Missouri River port from his native Germany. He was part of the westward movement that took place in the second half of the nineteenth century, joining pioneers, French trappers, and immigrants seeking a better life. Schwegmann, a successful miller, built a large brick Georgian-style home on the river-front in 1861, where he provided comfortable rooms for his preferred customers.

Travelers today can still enjoy this comfort with modern amenities added. Nine air-conditioned guest rooms offer a night's sleep amid formal antiques of that earlier era. Fires burn in the parlors' hearths on chilly evenings, and on warm days guests can relax on the patio or stroll in the gardens that overlook the Missouri River. A Continental breakfast of breads and croissants is accompanied by pots of local jams, imported cheeses, and local grape juice.

The inn's country store sells crafts, the inn's preserves, and baked goods and items reflecting the area's strong German influence. The Missouri River offers fishing, boating, and water skiing, while a nearby park has tennis and lake swimming. There are seven wineries within an easy drive of Washington, and Daniel Boone's home is in Defiance.

Accommodations: 9 rooms, 7 with private bath. *Pets:* Not permitted. *Driving Instructions:* From I-70 drive south 24 miles on Route 47; or from I-44, drive west 10 miles on Route 100.

Nebraska

FORT ROBINSON STATE PARK LODGE AND CABINS
  P.O. Box 392, Crawford, NB 69339. 308-665-2660. *Innkeeper:*
  Vince Rotherham. Open Memorial Day through Labor Day and
  on a limited basis thereafter until mid-November.

On September 5, 1877, a proud Indian chief was being led to impris-
onment in a small log cabin at Fort Robinson. Suddenly he struggled
free, slashing the hand of one of his captors. In an instant another
trooper from the fort thrust forward his bayonet, and it found its
mark. Thus died the greatest Oglala Sioux chief of recent history,
Chief Crazy Horse. The killing of Crazy Horse was but one in a long
string of encounters between the army troops and the local Sioux. For
many years Fort Robinson remained an important outpost in the de-
veloping Nebraska Territory. After World War II it was abandoned
by the army and taken over by the State of Nebraska. Today it serves
as the center of a state park that includes not only lodging in the many
historic fort buildings but several important museums and historical
sites.

  Overnight lodging is available in a variety of buildings dating from
the late-nineteenth and early-twentieth centuries. The largest facility
is the lodge, formerly the enlisted men's barracks, built in 1909. The
lodge is a two-and-one-half-story brick building with first- and
second-floor verandas running the length of the building and bound-
ed by tall columns. The lodge contains twenty-four guest rooms, and
a number of cabins on the grounds may be rented by families or
groups. The oldest of these are the Adobe Cabins, which date from
1874 and 1875, and the 1887 Officers Quarters. These are housekeeping cabins with baths, utensils, linens, dishes, and silverware

service for six. They range from two-bedroom to four-bedroom units. Several other cabins, with and without housekeeping facilities, are from the 1909 building programs and are constructed of brick. The largest are seven-bedroom units and are frequently rented by large groups. A modern campsite area is also on the grounds.

A popular attraction at the park is the Post Playhouse. The theater group presents a season of repertory that includes melodramas (recently presented were *Time Wounds All Heels* and *Frontier Fury, or Treachery at Fort Robinson*) and comedies. *Trailside Museum*, on the park grounds, shows the natural history of the area. The Fort Robinson Museum covers the area's history from prehistoric man through the Indian wars. Displays include the world's largest army remount depot, an adjutant's office, a guardhouse, and wheelwright, blacksmith, and harness repair shops. The museum is open all year, although on a limited basis in winter. In addition to these attractions, there are trail rides, jeep rides, several organized tours, stagecoach rides, cookouts, and weekly rodeos.

The dining room in the main lodge serves three meals daily to guests and the public. The menu includes buffalo cooked in many imaginative ways: tacos, buffalo pizza, stew, and steak.

Accommodations: 24 lodge rooms with private bath. Many cabins on the grounds. *Driving Instructions:* Fort Robinson is 3½ miles west of Crawford on Route 20.

North Dakota

Medora, North Dakota

Medora was founded in 1883 when the Marquis de Mores, a French nobleman, cracked a bottle of champagne over a tent peg and proclaimed that the town would forever bear the name of his daughter Medora. De Mores had come to the area earlier to hunt buffalo and bear, as did a more famous American, Theodore Roosevelt. Camped on the banks of the Little Missouri River, de Mores had envisioned an empire that would make him millions almost overnight. He built a meat-packing plant and started to ship dressed beef to stores he opened in large U.S. cities. (Some have speculated that he planned to use the profits to corrupt the French Army and restore the monarchy with himself as emperor.) His first packing plant was completed in October 1883, but his warehouse butchers began to report back to him that the consumers were complaining about the grass-fed beef. Rumors began to spread that his beef contained poisonous preservatives, and in 1886 he slaughtered his last herd. The winter that followed was one of the most grueling in North Dakota history. Many ranchers, including Roosevelt, were nearly or entirely wiped out. By the 1890s Medora was little more than a ghost town.

ROUGH RIDERS HOTEL

1 Main Street, Medora, North Dakota. Mailing address: P.O. Box 198, Medora, ND 58645. 701-623-4433. *Innkeeper:* Doug Jensen. Open May 15 to September 15.

Built in the 1880s to accommodate the cowboys and ranchers frequenting Medora, this two-story hotel still bears the brands burned

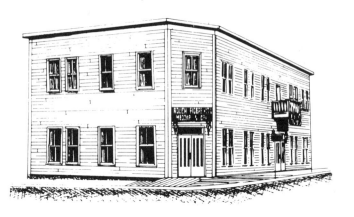

into its outside walls by exuberant cattlemen. The well-preserved, rough-sawed cedar building was one of the first restoration projects of the Gold Seal Company following its acquisition of much of the property in the old ghost town. When Teddy Roosevelt was in Medora as a young rancher in the Badlands, he would stay at the Rough Riders Hotel when he wasn't using his rooms above the town store. Most of the original furnishings survived intact through the seventy years that intervened between the building of the hotel and its restoration in the early 1960s. This furniture, carefully sandblasted, is in daily use at the hotel. Among the modern conveniences in the hotel's guest rooms, which otherwise retain an authentic old-West flavor, are wall-to-wall carpeting, air conditioning, modern bathrooms, and telephones. The building's unfinished horizontal cedar siding and simplicity of lines create an authentic Western setting that is free from commercialization.

The dining room at the Rough Riders offers a selection of beef that is appropriate to a hotel in a town that was founded to be a beef-packing center. Among the offerings are rib eye steak, tenderloin, barbecued back ribs, beef and shrimp kabob, and chopped buffalo steak. Roast buffalo and elk are available from time to time. Also on the menu are rainbow trout and lemon-baked chicken. All meals include salad, choice of vegetable or potato, and bread.

Accommodations: 9 rooms with private bath. *Driving Instructions:* Medora is about 30 miles west of Dickinson on I-94.

South Dakota

BLUE BELL LODGE AND RESORT

Custer State Park, Custer, SD 57730. 605-255-4531. *Innkeeper:* Phil Lampert. Open May 15 through September.

The Blue Bell Lodge is a fine old rustic lodge with log cabins scattered nearby in the seclusion of the ponderosa pines country of the mountainous Custer State Park. The lodge, at an elevation of 5,000 feet in the heart of the park's buffalo grounds, is owned by the state and leased on concession to Phil Lampert, a South Dakotan whose own living quarters are on the lodge's second floor.

The Blue Bell provides seventeen chinked-log cabins, eleven of which were built at the same time as the main lodge was, in 1920. The cabins are widely separated to ensure privacy. The older cabins are the smallest, have exposed-log walls inside, and contain heavy handmade pine furnishings in keeping with the atmosphere of a hunting lodge. Each has one room, housekeeping facilities, and heat. The cabins with kitchenettes do not come with dishes and utensils.

The main lodge is constructed inside and out of large ponderosa pine logs. The walls and 13-foot ceilings are of exposed chinked logs, and many animal trophies and stretched skins of local animals such as bison, elk, and deer are mounted on the walls. The building contains a lounging area for guests, a cocktail lounge, and a rough-log dining room warmed by a large stone fireplace with a log mantle. A trophy

elk head peers down from the hearth wall amid many other mounted trophies. The room is lit by the hearth fires and the lights in the wagon-wheel chandeliers, part of the original decor. A nearby rustic pine log building is ideal for reunions, banquets, and meetings.

Meals are served family-style to both lodgers and the public. The dining room offers breakfast, lunch, and dinner; the cocktail lounge is open for before- and after-dinner drinks. The menu features Black Hills mountain trout, fresh from a local stream, and buffalo meat or roast beef. Home-baked pastries top off the meals.

A gift shop in the lodge offers gifts and craft objects — many, such as the Black Hills gold jewelry, are made locally of Black Hills materials. Innkeeper Phil Lampert specializes in buffalo trophies of all sorts, and he sells robes, skins, heads, and skulls in the shop. Guided trail rides, hayrides, and chuckwagon cookouts are all popular with guests. The lodge is centrally located in relation to most of the Black Hills attractions.

Accommodations: 17 cabins with private bath. *Driving Instructions:* The lodge is 42 miles south of Rapid City on Route 87, in the heart of Custer State Park. It is 12 miles from Custer and 25 miles from Hot Springs.

The Rockies

Arizona

Bisbee, Arizona

Bisbee, "Queen of the Mining Camps," sits on a mile-high plateau in the southeastern corner of Arizona. The county, Cochise, was named for the famous Chiricahua Apache chief who led his people in war against the United States for more than a decade in the late nineteenth century. The town of Bisbee was built with the copper fortunes made here from the most productive mines the West has ever seen. Bisbee is a history buff's and shutterbug's delight. The historic town is built on canyon walls and the sides of steep hills, and it appears much the same today as it was in the raucous days of the wild West. In addition to the restored *Copper Queen Hotel*, the town has reopened the *Copper Queen Mines*, where visitors are outfitted with yellow slickers and miners' lights and led through a series of tunnels and shafts while guides explain the operations. The tour ends with a mine train ride to the outside. This tour is not for claustrophobes, but it is certainly thrilling. *The Lavender Pit* is out in the open air, where tourists can see a huge open pit mine. *Brewery Gulch* is just around the corner from the Copper Queen Hotel. The gulch, named for Muheim's Brewery, at one time boasted forty bars and a great number of ladies of the evening.

COPPER QUEEN HOTEL

11 Howell Street, Bisbee, Arizona. Mailing address: P.O. Box Drawer CQ, Bisbee, AZ 85603. 602-432-2216. *Innkeepers:* Richard and Virginia Hort. Open all year.

The Copper Queen Hotel, once considered the finest hotel in the West, is named for the most productive and famous underground copper mine. Since the gigantic copper finds of the 1870s the town has been known as the "Queen of the Mining Camps." Shortly after the turn of the century, the huge, wealthy Copper Mining Camp (later merged to become the Phelps Dodge Corporation) built the Copper Queen Hotel to house the many mining executives, traveling salesmen in the copper business, territorial governors, and flamboyant characters attracted to this boom town.

The Copper Queen Properties purchased the old hotel and have restored it to its heyday. This restoration is an ongoing project, with very successful results so far. The original furnishings have received face-lifts; the hotel looks not like a restoration but as if it had never changed. Guests enter the ground-floor lobby and sign in at the front desk with its creaky old cash register and original switchboard. The sturdy Victor Safe is guarded by the handsome wall clock above it, its pendulum still marking time as it has since the hotel's beginnings. The furnishings of this room and the second floor guest lounge are pure "1920s–1930s hotel." The large pieces of furniture are leather-cushioned and ornately carved wood.

The rooms throughout are furnished with antiques and "near antiques" of the 1920s through the 1940s. The forty-three guest rooms vary from spacious, high-ceiling affairs to intimate little nests. All of the rooms have private baths or showers; some have the old claw-footed tubs. The previous owner, in a burst of enthusiasm for the color red, papered the upper floors with flocked red bordello-style wallpaper and laid down a great deal of shaggy red carpeting.

The Copper Queen Saloon and Dining Room are off either side of the lobby. The saloon has a nostalgic bar and many cartoon sketches of local characters past and present as well as of celebrities who have appeared here while on location for the many films shot in town. The dining room has blue and white gingham checkered tablecloths, period decor, and tall windows looking out to the mountains across the street. The menu features Western-style meals of steaks, ribs, and poultry. A favorite is duckling. The dessert specialty is a homemade carrot cake. The hotel serves three meals a day to guests and public alike. Both the saloon and the dining room offer liquor and a selection of wines.

Accommodations: 43 rooms with private bath. *Pets:* Not allowed. *Driving Instructions:* The town is 95 miles southeast of Tucson. Take I-10 east to Route 80, then Route 80 to Bisbee.

Bisbee, Arizona

THE INN AT CASTLE ROCK

112 Tombstone Canyon, Bisbee, Arizona. Mailing address: P.O. Box 1161, Bisbee, AZ 85603. 602-432-7195. *Innkeeper:* Dorothy Pearl. Open all year.

Bisbee is a mining town built on the mountainsides and canyons in the Mule Mountains. The Inn at Castle Rock was a miners' boarding house built at the turn of the century in Tombstone Canyon. It clings to the steep canyon walls facing Castle Rock across the way, which is viewed from a large guest lounge with a hearth and period furnishings. The inn was over a mine shaft that later filled with water. The shaft is now a centerpiece of the guest parlor, which has natural rock walls, a fireplace, Mexican tilework, and plants. Goldfish swim in the well.

Dorothy Pearl serves breakfast in the Victorian dining room or out in the garden. Guests can stroll in the rock gardens set in the steep hillside that goes practically straight up behind the inn. A narrow footbridge leads from the upper stories of the inn to terraced gardens and an Indian ramada with a hammock. Guest rooms range from intimate little rooms simply furnished in a variety of antique styles to an art deco room and a Victorian-style room with a brass bed and marble-topped tables.

Accommodations: 12 rooms, 10 with private bath. *Driving Instructions:* From Tucson, take I-10 east to the Benson exit, then go south on Route 80 to Bisbee. In town, take Main Street north through town, where it becomes the Tombstone Canyon road. The inn is on the left.

Cochise, Arizona

Cochise is a small town in the heart of the former Apache stronghold about 85 miles east of Tucson and 65 miles north of the Mexican border. As you drive through the area, the exploits of the Western heroes of the dime novels of yesterday seem to live again behind every rock and over every ridge. About 15 miles to the northeast is the town of Willcox, site of the *Cochise Visitor Center.* The museum contains important exhibits relating to the Apache Indian heritage and the history and culture of Cochise County. From Cochise one can take a one- or two-day circular tour of Cochise County that includes the old copper-mining town of Bisbee; Tombstone, the town that wouldn't die; and the border town of Douglas. The Amerind Foundation in Dragoon operates a museum of the arts, crafts, archaeology, and history of the prehistoric and historic Indians of all the Americas. Open by appointment only on weekends, when free tours are given. 602-586-3003.

COCHISE HOTEL

Cochise Road, Cochise, AZ. Mailing address: Box 27, Cochise, AZ 85606. 602-384-3156. *Innkeeper:* Mrs. Thomas B. Husband. Lillie Harrington, manager. Open all year by reservation only.

If you happen to have a Wells Fargo stagecoach at your disposal, you will in no way feel out of place arriving at the Cochise Hotel. Built in 1882 of thick adobe, the hotel stands at the former junction of the Southern Pacific and old Arizona Eastern railways. The long front hallway contained the Wells Fargo office that handled the ore shipments from the Johnson and Pearce mines of an era gone by.

Cross the threshold of the Cochise Hotel today and you are transported back to turn-of-the-century Arizona. The furnishings are authentic pieces from the nineteenth century: a wind-up phonograph, heavy walnut tables and chairs, rocking chairs, a carved wooden sofa upholstered in tan velvet (reputed to have belonged to Jenny Lind), a large wardrobe with mirrored doors, and other pieces of the period all arranged with formality around an Oriental carpet. A painted china and brass chandelier with dropping crystal pendants and period table lamps add their glow.

The five guest rooms carry out the period theme with furnishings that provide comfort while at the same time preserving the earlier era.

Each guest room has had a modern bathroom and heating installed, but the improvements are in no way intrusive. The menu in the dining room is a simple one. With the exception of breakfast, meals include a choice of broiled steak or chicken and are served family style, with vegetables, potatoes, hot rolls, and dessert. All meals are by reservation only.

Accommodations: 5 rooms with private bath. *Pets:* Permitted by special arrangement only. *Driving Instructions:* Take I-10 to Route 666, then drive south 5 miles to Cochise Road.

Douglas, Arizona

Douglas, a border town of 12,000 in the extreme southeastern corner of the state, is a good stopover for people who wish to explore the *Coronado National Forest* and *Chiricahua National Monument* to the northeast and Tombstone and the *Cochise Stronghold Recreation Area* to the northwest. The Stronghold was the hiding place of the great Apache chief for many years in the late nineteenth century. Douglas offers easy access to the Mexican city of Agua Prieta, just across the border in Sonora. One day's travel to such border cities as Agua Prieta is an easy matter. No special permits are required for U.S. citizens, provided they go no more than 15 miles into Mexico. Most Mexican stores will gladly accept U.S. currency, so money need not be exchanged. Visitors traveling in and out of Mexico are advised to leave luggage at their U.S. hotel or inn because the presence of luggage will be likely to cause serious delays for custom checks. For extended trips beyond the border, consult your nearest Mexican tourist agency or Mexican Consulate for detailed travel information. The U.S. Customs Office, Washington, D.C. 20226, also has useful travel information about passing through customs with minimal delay. Its free pamphlets outline what may be brought across the border legally and without customs duty.

GADSDEN HOTEL

1046 G Avenue West, Douglas, AZ 85607. 602-364-4481. *Innkeepers:* Marjorie and Russell Madsen. Open all year.

The Gadsden is a classic southwestern hotel built under the inspired direction of an Italian architect in 1927 to replace an old wood-frame hotel that had stood on the same site. The present five-story building bears some elaborate ornamentation on its exterior, but it is in the lobby that the scope and magnitude of the Italianate design are most apparent. In the middle of the lobby is a wide set of marble stairs, which mount to the fifth floor. At the mezzanine level, a huge stained-glass depiction of a desert scene sparkles in the daylight, as bright today as it was in 1930, when it was installed by Tiffany's of New York. From the center of the lobby rise large polished marble columns decorated at their tops with solid gold leaf. Gold leaf continues across the entire ceiling, broken only by two stained-glass sunlights, also by Tiffany's.

In addition to the hotel's lobby, the Saddle and Spur Lounge is distinctive, with walls bearing the brands of more than 2000 ranches from all over the world. The backbar is the original, fashioned from cherry wood, but the rest of the room has been modernized over the years. The dining room is in a classic Spanish motif, with ornate carved wood and the original Spanish murals.

The 147 guest rooms and four suites are on the four floors above, with no two rooms alike. These rooms have benefitted from a $500,000, three-year renovation. Many have Spanish-style furnishings and decor. The bathrooms have the original handmade Mexican tiles and modern fixtures.

Accommodations: 147 rooms with private bath; 4 suites. *Driving Instructions:* The hotel, in downtown Douglas, 1 1/2 miles from the border, can be reached from either Route 80 or Route 666.

ARIZONA MOUNTAIN INN

685 Lake Mary Road, Flagstaff, AZ 86001. 602-774-8959. *Innkeepers:* Ray and Pauline Wanek and family. Open all year.

In 1947 Ray Wanek decided to leave home to seek a new life as a homesteader in Alaska. He got as far as northern Arizona when he said "This is it!" and started to build his first log-and-stone cabin just outside of Flagstaff. He hasn't been to Alaska yet.

Over the years Wanek constructed a total of 16 beam-ceilinged chalets and cottages, usually completing each new cottage in one summer. In 1980 he and his wife Pauline undertook their most ambitious project yet — a 7,000-square-foot, Tudor-style passive solar home. As they had always done in the past, they used as many indigenous building materials as possible. Ponderosa pine logs from the nearby forest were cut with a portable saw. Ray took his jeep to Dry Beaver Creek almost every day one winter to gather white, river-polished sandstone, later incorporated into a large interior wall along which a striking banistered staircase rises. The inn has five fireplaces with mantels carved by Argentine craftsmen. Antique furnishings have been used throughout, augmented by examples of hand-carved glass, products of Pauline's father, Joseph Cummings, who has also created art glass for Steuben. The inn's honeymoon suite has a 6-foot hot tub and a Jacuzzi. As one stands surrounded by the Cococino National Forest with views of the San Francisco mountain peaks, it is difficult to remember that these 13 acres are but two miles from the city of Flagstaff.

The Waneks offer a country-style breakfast in the dining room, generally with a choice of meats, eggs, home-baked breads, coconut pancakes, or French toast. Honeymooners are served in bed. Complimentary wine and cheese is served near the large stone living room fireplace in the early evening.

Accommodations: 5 rooms, 2 with private bath, and 16 housekeeping cottages and chalets with up to 5 bedrooms, all with 1 or 2 baths. *Driving Instructions:* From I-17, take Lake Mary Road 1 mile southeast to the Inn.

THE MINER'S ROOST

309 Main Street, Jerome, Arizona. Mailing address: P.O. Box 758, Jerome, AZ 86331. 602-634-5094. *Innkeepers:* Betty and George Daech. Open all year.

Jerome is a former mining town that clings precariously to a hillside overlooking the Verde Valley floor some 1500 feet below, looking much as it did a century ago during the town's boom days. Although many of its original wooden buildings have burned over the decades, those that remain form a living museum to the mining industry that thrived for more than seventy years, an industry that produced over $800,000,000 in copper, gold, and silver ores.

One such historic building is The Miner's Roost. Built in 1899, the building once housed Jerome's first telephone company. Later it served as a saloon, mortuary, hardware store, and real estate office. Today, the hotel occupies the second floor above the innkeeper's restaurant and bar, Betty's Ore House. Upstairs, a parlor—with leather sofa, oak sideboard, armchairs, and gas fireplace—is reserved for use by overnight guests. Guest rooms have been named for infamous "ladies" of the mining town and for some of Jerome's historic buildings. "Little Daisy," for example, gets its name from one of the largest hotels that once housed miners. Its walnut bedstead has a yellow puff and a paddle fan. "Jenny Banters" is a cozy Victorian-style room with a working Victrola. Downstairs, a recently added oak-paneled bar is a popular gathering spot.

Betty's Ore House offers a variety of breakfast and luncheon dishes, including *huevos rancheros,* build-your-own omelets, assorted club sandwiches and hamburgers, quiche lorraine, and several vegetarian dishes. After 5:00 P.M., Betty's supplements the luncheon menu with several dinner specials, which are posted on the cafe's blackboard.

Accommodations: 6 rooms with shared bath. *Pets and children:* Not permitted. *Driving Instructions:* Highway 89A becomes Main Street. The hotel is on the north side.

Paradise Valley, Arizona

Paradise Valley is, along with Scottsdale, a part of the northeastern suburban core of Phoenix. As with all urban areas represented in this book, space does not permit a thorough discussion of area attractions. A representative selection: *The Phoenix Art Museum* is a fine, wide-ranging museum with collections representing North America, Europe, and the Orient. It is at 1625 North Central Avenue and is open daily except Mondays; there is no charge for admission. The *Heard Museum of Anthropology and Primitive Arts* is a major center for Indian displays and arts and crafts exhibits. The museum is at 22 East Monte Vista Road; it is open daily with nominal admission charges. The *Phoenix Zoo* at 60th Street and East Van Buren has a worldwide collection of animals. It is open daily and an admission is charged. The *Desert Botanical Garden* in Papago Park, with access from 58th Street and Van Buren or 64th Street and McDowell, contains more than a thousand different cacti and other unusual plants in a natural setting. For further area information contact the Phoenix and Valley of the Sun Convention and Visitors Bureau, 2701 East Camelback Road, Phoenix, AZ 85061.

HERMOSA INN

5592 North Palo Cristi Road, Paradise Valley, AZ 85253. 602-955-8614. *Innkeeper:* Harold "Red" Frey. Open all year.
The Hermosa Inn has an interesting history that dates back about fifty years. In 1930, cowboy-artist Lon Megargee completed his Casa Hermosa (handsome house), a rambling Spanish-Colonial hacienda. The structure, typical of Megargee's style of life and painting, was constructed without formal blueprints and guided only by inspiration. Scion of an old Philadelphia family, exhibition roper, rancher, town fireman, and poker dealer, Megargee was a self-taught artist who gained considerable fame. He did a series of paintings for the Arizona Capitol and later became famous for two paintings commissioned by an Arizona brewery: *Black Bart* and *Cowboy's Dream*. As Megargee's hacienda gradually expanded through the addition of other buildings, he decided to convert his residence into a guest ranch. A few years later he sold out and moved on.

What he left behind was a beautiful main lodge and individual guest cottages. Many of the original structural features—including secret

passages, beehive fireplaces, massive doors, and handsome iron work—remain today. From its tiled roof to the adobe turrets to its heavy beams and wooden ceilings, the building's effect is a blend of Mexican and Spanish rustic. Accommodations are thoroughly modern, and they were recently remodeled. Each room has combination tub and shower, color television, telephone, and private patio. Guest facilities range from rooms with queen-size or two double beds, to efficiencies in the casitas, to villa suites with living room, kitchen, two bedrooms, and two bathrooms. On the grounds are three tennis courts (with a tennis pro), a heated pool, and a Jacuzzi. The ten newest units have Jacuzzis and wet bars.

Accommodations: 51 units and suites with private bath. *Pets:* Not permitted. *Driving Instructions:* The inn is on Palo Cristi Road (also called Thirty-sixth Street), south of its intersection with Lincoln Drive in Paradise Valley.

Prescott, Arizona

HASSAYAMPA INN

122 East Gurley Street, Prescott, Arizona. Mailing address: P.O. Box 2356, Prescott, AZ 86302. 602-778-9434. *Innkeeper:* George Lee. Open all year.

Franciscan-motif ceiling frescos, overstuffed leather sofas, potted palms, Oriental rugs, and an original birdcage elevator staffed by a uniformed bellman are all reminiscent of the Jazz Age of the 1920s—of prohibition, bootleggers, and flappers. Built in 1927 to the Pueblo Art Deco design of southwestern architect Henry C. Trost, the Hassayampa was treated to a multimillion-dollar restoration in 1985. Enough of the hotel's original Castillian walnut and tile furnishings survived to outfit about half the guest rooms. Fine Belgian and English fabrics have been used throughout, and telephones and television sets have been discretely fitted into all guest rooms.

The hotel's bar, dining rooms, and meeting room all have outstanding etched-glass panels by master-craftsman Bill Stephenson of Phoenix. The dining room serves three meals daily to guests and the public. The evening menu changes from time to time, but frequently includes such offerings as trout stuffed with scallops, crabmeat, and shrimp, broiled fresh swordfish, steak au poivre, veal with peppercorns, or roast duckling.

Accommodations: 67 rooms with private bath. *Pets:* Not permitted. *Driving Instructions:* Take either Route 89 or 69 to Prescott. From the center of town, turn at the Court House onto Gurley. The inn is on the north side, between Cortez and Marina.

HOTEL VENDOME

230 South Cortez Street, Prescott, AZ 86301. 602-776-0900. *Innkeeper:* Janie Stamp. Open all year.

Mile-high Prescott, surrounded by Ponderosa pines and the Bradshaw Mountains, is near Flagstaff and Phoenix and is just a short drive from the red-rock country of Sedona. The Hotel Vendome is a restored 1917 boardinghouse with brass ceiling fans, tiled baths, cable televison, and queen-size beds. The rooms have reproduction oak furnishings and old-fashioned tiny-print wallpapers. In the lobby there is cherrywood bar. Some of the guest rooms have antique clawfooted tubs, and others have modern low tubs with built-in shelves for wine or champagne. A Continental breakfast is served to guests, and there are several good restaurants nearby.

Accommodations: 21 rooms with private bath. *Driving Instructions:* From Phoenix, drive north on I-17 to Cortez Junction (Route 69). Take Route 69 to Prescott and Route 89. Follow Gurley Street and turn left at the fifth light (Cortez Street). Go one block past the light (Goodwin Street). The inn is on the right.

Sedona, Arizona

L'AUBERGE DE SEDONA

301 Little Lane, Sedona, Arizona. Mailing address: P.O. Box B, Sedona, AZ 86336. 602-282-1661; toll free: 800-272-6776 (outside Arizona). *Innkeeper:* Jean Rocchi. Open all year.

Guests can enjoy a five-course French dinner at a restaurant in a desert canyon and then, after a stroll under the stars, return to a wisteria-covered cottage filled with French antiques. At L'Auberge de Sedona, there are decorated canopied beds with designs from the studios of Pierre Deux, thick carpets, and fires in the stone fireplaces.

Upon waking, overnight guests can step into a private garden patio or onto a deck to hear the rushing water of the mountain stream that carved Oak Creek Canyon, whose floor is a bower of tall trees and greenery, in stark contrast to the towering red-rock walls and buttes. The restaurant, decorated in pinks and greens, has balcony seating overlooking the creek and fresh flowers, French linens, and morning-glory-pattern china. Changing menu offerings, in the nouvelle French manner, might include duckling with Japanese plum sauce, loin of lamb with macadamia-chutney butter sauce, salmon with sorrel cream, and sea scallops with fresh ginger and lime. The grounds have flowering and fruit trees, and the historic community of Sedona, with its boutiques and art galleries, is an easy walk away.

Accommodations: 34 cottage rooms and 20 rooms in the lodge, all with private bath. *Pets:* Not permitted. *Driving Instructions:* The inn is on Route 89A, 1 block north of Route 179.

GARLAND'S OAK CREEK LODGE

Highway 89-A, Oak Creek Canyon, Sedona, AZ. Mailing address: Box 152, Sedona, AZ 86336. 602-282-3343. *Innkeepers:* Gary and Mary Garland. Open April to mid-November, except Sundays.

The Oak Creek Lodge is in the "prettiest spot in Arizona," on the Oak Creek in the canyon with its red-rock formations. The lodge, which began as a homestead at the turn of the century, is built of hand-hewn logs and today contains a dining room, a comfortable lounge with fireplace, and a kitchen. Guests stay in idyllic, rustic log cabins around a large lawn, English garden, and two ponds. Most of the one-room cabins feature handmade furniture and double beds. The largest log cabins have two beds and fireplaces for chilly evenings; the smaller cabins all have a double bed and overlook the Oak Creek.

The Garlands' property includes a working fruit orchard where apples, peaches, pears, and plums are grown. These, along with organically grown vegetables and the Garlands' own fresh eggs, the lodge's kitchen transforms into fine country-style meals emphasizing fresh, homemade foods. Breakfast and dinner are included in the room rates. The day begins with fresh-baked muffins, homemade preserves, and a featured main course—omelet, eggs any style, or waffles or pancakes—served with ham, bacon, or sausage. Soups, breads, salads, and desserts are prepared from scratch daily. A typical meal might include sorrel soup and Scotch oat bread, duck or fresh trout accompanied by organic tomatoes with Roquefort or a Portland spinach salad and stuffed zucchini, and an apple walnut pie or a pear-peach tart. Guests are seated at tables decorated with fresh flowers and old-fashioned oil lamps. Only one entrée is offered each night, and a selection of California wines is available with the meal.

Accommodations: 15 log cabins; 12 with two double beds, 3 with one double bed. *Pets:* Not permitted. *Driving Instructions:* 8 miles north of Sedona on Highway 89-A in Oak Creek Canyon, the lodge is 20 miles south of Flagstaff.

GRAHAM'S BED AND BREAKFAST

150 Canyon Circle Drive, Sedona, Arizona. Mailing address: P.O. Box 912, Sedona, AZ 86336. 602-284-1425. *Innkeepers:* Bill and Marni Graham. Open all year.

Sedona is high desert country; at the base of towering red rock formations sprawls Graham's Bed and Breakfast, surrounded by dramatic Red Rock scenery. Large picture windows bring the hills indoors. The living room has soft, comfortable seating, a fireplace, and reading material on the attractions of the area. Each guest room is quite individual. The Southwest Suite has hand-hewn log furnishings, a sofa by the working fireplace, and a large whirlpool tub in the bathroom. The Heritage Room is decorated in red, white, and blue with a brass bed and army memorabilia. The rooms have balconies overlooking the desert terrain. There is a tiled, heated swimming pool on the terrace. Breakfast is treated as a special event, with both Bill and Marni creating unusual treats.

Accommodations: 5 rooms with private bath. *Pets and smoking:* Not permitted. *Children:* Under 12 not permitted. *Driving Instructions:* In Sedona, take Route 179 to Bell Rock Boulevard. Turn west and proceed two blocks to Canyon Circle Drive. Turn right. The inn is on the left.

Tucson, Arizona

Tucson lies in a bowl-like depression surrounded by a ring of mountains and miles of desert. With an hour's drive one can leave the sweltering heat of the center of the city and be high in the mountains among the pines and snow in winter. Tucson is in the land of the saguaro, the stately cactus that perhaps best represents the outsider's notion of what a true desert should be. Among the area's diverse sights are the *San Xavier Mission*, which dates from the late eighteenth century; the *Arizona–Sonora Desert Museum*, where the visitor can see otters play in special glass-walled tanks, and numerous displays on desert life; and *Old Tucson*, a Western movie location *par excellence*. Within the city limits, the *Arizona Historical Society* at Second Street and Park Avenue and the *Tucson Museum of Art* at 235 West Alameda are logical stopping places for first-time visitors. For further area information, write the Tucson Convention and Visitors Bureau, 450 West Paseo Redondo, Tucson, AZ 85705. 602-624-1814.

ARIZONA INN

2200 East Elm Street, Tucson, AZ 85719. 602-325-1541. *Innkeeper:* John S. Greenway. Open all year.

Isabella Greenway, the first congresswoman from Arizona and a woman of great energy, envisioned a plan to rehabilitate World War I veterans. She oversaw the formation of a handmade-furniture guild that would provide the returning soldiers with a skill as well as a marketable product. By 1930 the plan had become so successful that she managed to furnish her newly constructed Arizona inn with some of the surplus from this craft endeavor as well as with many of her personal effects.

The Arizona Inn today consists of a series of adobe-style cottages with private bath set on 14 acres of landscaped grounds. Each guest room is furnished individually with a selection of the family's antiques and handmade furniture. The inn's guest lounge has a beamed ceiling, large fireplace, antique furniture, and Moroccan rugs. The walls display a selection of George Catlin and Audubon lithographs.

The Arizona Inn prides itself on personal attention to guests starting with breakfast and ending with after-dinner drinks, pehaps before a wood fire in the lounge fireplace on a winter evening. The dining room, considered one of the best in Tucson, offers about ten entrées

that change regularly. Typical selections include veal piccata au champignons, shrimp à la Greque, broiled filet mignon, and baked cabrilla San Carlos. Special diets can be arranged by the chef, just one example of how the inn looks after its guests' individual needs. Guests at the inn have included John D. Rockefeller, Cary Grant, and the Duke and Duchess of Windsor. More than likely, you will be as pleased with the food and service as they were. And it's nice company to keep.

Accommodations: 85 rooms with private bath. *Pets:* Not permitted. *Driving Instructions:* From Phoenix, take I-10 to the Speedway Boulevard exit. Go east on Speedway past the University of Arizona, turn left on Campbell, drive five blocks, then turn right on Elm Street.

HACIENDA DEL SOL

5601 North, Hacienda del Sol Road, Tucson, AZ 85718. 602-299-1501. Open all year.

The Hacienda del Sol is an elegant ranch resort in the Southwest. The old adobe structure is in a high-style Mexican form with stucco arches, heavy, dark exposed beams, and a collection of decorative Mexican and Indian art, accessories, and handicrafts. In addition to the original buildings there are several cottage-casitas, a tennis court, an enclosed therapy pool, and an exercise room. Guests have a choice of accommodations. There are large suites with living rooms and fireplaces, some with kitchenettes and private patios. Other rooms are of varying sizes and locations, with views of mountains, sunsets, the city, or the garden courtyards. Each public room has large stuccoed walls broken by broad expanses of glass offering vistas of the surrounding desert or the Catalina Mountains. Many doorways are accented with hand-painted tiles, and the doors themselves bear the Spanish look of heavy panels. Meals are available.

Accommodations: 43 rooms with private bath. *Pets:* Not permitted. *Driving Instructions:* Take I-10 to Prince Road, then drive east to Campbell Road, north to River Road, and east to Hacienda del Sol Road. Drive north on that road.

THE LODGE ON THE DESERT

306 North Alvernon Way, Tucson, AZ. Mailing address: Box 42500, Tucson, AZ 85711. 602-325-3366. *Innkeeper:* Schuyler W. Lininger. Open all year.

The Lodge on the Desert is styled after a Mexican hacienda, and the decor throughout is completely under the Mexican-Spanish influence. The lodge was started by the parents of the present innkeeper and was his family home for many years. Over the years, it has gradually expanded from its original nine rooms to its present forty guest rooms plus a number of public rooms.

The orientation at the lodge is toward outdoor living. Even inside, one has a lovely view of the Santa Catalina mountains to the north. The feeling of old Mexico and the flavor of the Southwest are captured within the patio walls of the lodge. There are adobe-colored *casas* with their ocotillo-covered porches, intimate Spanish court-yards, spacious lawns, and flower-filled gardens. Inside, the heavy original beams and broad expanses of plastered walls, exposed wooden lintels over the windows, and tin chandeliers enhance the hacienda feeling.

The guest rooms, like the public rooms, have a Spanish look. More than half of the guest rooms have their own wood-burning fireplaces, and all have their own tiled bathrooms.

The lodge takes special pride in its food service. Breakfasts, from a menu with several choices, are cooked to order and delivered to guest rooms at no additional charge. Lunch and dinner are served in the Mexican tiled dining rooms, one of which is noted for its fluted Mexican fireplace. When the American Plan is in effect (during the cooler months), the dining room offers a limited menu with four entrées at lunch and four at dinner. A typical selection of lunch choices might include french fried turkey with almond sauce, broccoli supreme, beef tostado, and baked ham loaf with mustard sauce. Quiche is a frequent luncheon choice. Dinners are always preceded by a homemade soup such as spinach and oyster soup, Chantilly soup, or the Lodge on the Desert special "glorified" chicken soup. Entrée choices usually include a daily roast such as lamb, loin of pork, or beef, or chicken Maryland with horseradish sauce, fillet of sole bonne femme, or veal parmesan with fettuccini.

Accommodations: 40 rooms with private bath. *Pets:* Inquire first. *Driving Instructions:* The lodge is in the center of Tucson, about 2 miles east of the University of Arizona campus. Take Broadway east from I-10 about 4 miles to North Alvernon and go north to the lodge.

KAY EL BAR RANCH

Rincon Road, Box 2480, Wickenburg, AZ 85358. 602-684-7593.
Innkeeper: Jane Nash. Open mid-October through April.

On the Hassayampa River, which flows underground most of the year, the Kay el Bar nestles in a little desert valley surrounded by trees and grass. It was built as a working ranch in the early 1900s, on property that was a Spanish land grant before statehood was bestowed on Arizona. In 1926 it became a dude ranch offering Western food, horseback riding, and recreational facilities for the whole family. Its peaceful surroundings are populated by all sorts of wildlife and many domestic animals. The Kay el Bar is a National Historic Site because of its original adobe buildings, whose 18-inch-thick walls are in excellent condition today.

On cool nights, fires blaze in the stone fireplaces in the recreation and dining rooms of the ranch lodge. Guests like to relax with a game of cards or have a drink at the bar. All meals are served only to ranch guests, in the dining room with its stone hearth. Specialties include steaks, barbequed ribs, and chicken, accompanied by homemade breads, beans, and fried apples.

In addition to offering trail riding across thousands of acres of desert, the Kay el Bar has outdoor recreations such as swimming in the heated pool, volleyball, horseshoes, table tennis, and shuffleboard.

Accommodations: 10 rooms with private bath. *Pets:* Not permitted. *Driving Instructions:* Take I-89/93 into Wickenburg, and follow the signs to the ranch (3 miles from town).

Colorado

Aspen, Colorado

HOTEL JEROME

330 East Main Street, Aspen, CO 81611. 800-331-7213 from outside Colorado; 800-423-0037 from Colorado. *Innkeeper:* Jean Loubat. Open all year.

Aspen is now a year-round resort in a mountain setting. The Hotel Jerome, built in 1880 by Jerome Wheeler, president of Macy's, to rival the Hotel Ritz in Paris, has been restored to provide lodging and dining on a scale to match the mountain setting. The 27-room Hotel Jerome offers the amenities of a modern hotel in a Victorian of setting. The rooms and suites are furnished with restored period antiques, artwork, and velvets, silks, and crocheted laces. Antique armoires house television sets and minibars. Each spacious bathroom has a Jacuzzi. The staff can to arrange a variety of services, including babysitters, theater tickets, restaurant reservations, and secretarial services. The hotel offers complementary shuttle service to the airport.

For meals, there is a choice of dining rooms: the formal Silver Queen for candlelit French dinners, a comfortable tea room for breakfast and lunch, and Jacobs Corner, a casual breakfast and brunch spot with light meals. Some boast that the old-fashioned Jerome Bar is one of the best ski bars in the country.

Accommodations: 27 rooms with private bath. *Pets:* Not permitted. *Driving Instructions:* From Glenwood Springs, take Route 82 to Aspen.

Boulder, Colorado

BRIAR ROSE BED AND BREAKFAST

2151 Arapahoe, Boulder, CO 80302. 303-442-3007. *Innkeeper:* Emily Hunter. Open all year.

Built about 1904, Briar Rose is a Victorian brick home with eleven guest rooms. Now restored, it has received an Award of Merit by the Boulder Historical Society. Like the building, the guest rooms have a style that springs from its graceful simplicity. One of the rooms in the East Wing, for example, has a matched pair of mahogany Queen Anne chairs, a queen-size bed topped with a floral pattern comforter, a free-standing, wood-frame mirror, and a working fireplace. An East Wing bedroom has a queen-size bed tucked into an alcove and, again, a fireplace adds romance. Complimentary sherry and afternoon tea are served in the living room, where a fire burns on chilly evenings. All through summer and fall, the porch is festooned with bunches of drying flowers for the potpourri that is one of Emily Hunter's specialties. On the last Sunday of each month, the inn hosts a high tea, at which a classical ensemble or pianist performs. During intermission, tea, coffee, scones, cucumber sandwiches, fruit, and tarts are served. Many of these same treats appear each morning with the complimentary Continental breakfast.

Accommodations: 11 rooms, 6 with private bath. *Driving Instructions:* From Denver, take Route 36 to Boulder. Turn left on Arapahoe Avenue at the Crossroads Shopping Center. The inn is on the right just past the intersection of Arapahoe and 22nd Street.

PEARL STREET INN

1820 Pearl Street, Boulder, CO 80302. 303-444-5584. *Innkeeper:* Yossi Shem-Avi. Open all year.

Pearl Street Inn tries to provide overnight guests with the services of a luxury hotel combined with the comforts of a small inn. There are working fireplaces, private tiled baths, and phones in the rooms. Down comforters are turned down at night, and chocolates are left on pillows. A full bar and in-room catering services are available. The bedrooms are furnished with antiques and offer views of the garden courtyard. Sherry is served hearthside in the living room overlooking the front court. In warm weather, chilled wines and iced tea can be enjoyed under fruit trees on the rear courtyard. Light Continental breakfasts are served here or in the dining room. The enclosed garden courtyard offers peace and seclusion, but the inn is within walking distance of many boutiques, restaurants, and sights.

Accommodations: 8 rooms with private bath. *Driving Instructions:* From Denver, take I-25 north and exit onto Route 36 (Denver-Boulder Turnpike). Follow the turnpike into Boulder. It will merge into 28 Street. Turn left at Pearl Street.

Colorado Springs, Colorado

THE HEARTHSTONE INN
    506 North Cascade Avenue, Colorado Springs, CO 80903. 303-473-4413. *Innkeepers:* Ruth Williams and Dorothy Williams. Open all year.

The Hearthstone Inn is a Queen Anne mansion in the Rockies. The elaborate building is trimmed in lavender, peach, plum, and bittersweet—all authentic Victorian colors. It was built in 1885 by the Bemis family, and the decorative detailing is still intact. After being a private home, it became a boardinghouse, then an apartment building. In 1977 Dorothy and Ruth Williams found the run-down structure and set about the task of complete and authentic restoration, converting it into an inn. The mansion is listed in the National Register of Historic Places.

    In 1982 Ruth and Dot were able to acquire the turn-of-the-century home next door, and they painstakingly restored it to include a dining facility much larger than that in the mansion, as well as eleven additional guest rooms. The original carriage house, complete with open rafters, was moved to snuggle between the two buildings and form a sitting-room link connecting the homes. An oaken pump organ, which was exhibited at the 1893 Columbian Exposition, is in the carriage house, inviting anyone to sit down and play.

Each room, hallway, or landing has its distinctive wallpaper and decor. Dot and Ruth put up *all* the wallpaper (792 rolls), and the curtains (for all 124 windows) were made by Ruth's mother. The elaborate walnut beds and marble-topped dressers, hand-carved cherry headboards, and ornate sofas all came from the Midwest. The mansion is filled with authentic brass lighting fixtures and pots of greenery.

It would be difficult to pick a favorite guest accommodation here; each has its own special features, color combination, and name. The bedroom of the Study Suite, on the ground floor, has a large working fireplace, a window seat, a queen-size brass bed, and an adjoining room with twin beds. Fireside is a very large room, with another working fireplace, a king-size iron-and-brass bed, and a private balcony, where breakfast can be served outdoors. The seven third-floor rooms—with such names as Peak View, the Loft, and Solitude—all have slanted ceilings and quaint dormers with inset windows. All of the rooms have oak, walnut, or cherry beds and dressers, marble-topped tables, and washstands, some with the original china bowls and pitchers. The Solarium, on the second floor, a favorite of honeymooners, has a secluded little porch with a view of the mountains.

Mornings in the Hearthstone Inn are a treat. Breakfasts, included in the room rate, are served in the sunny dining room, with a fire in the fireplace if the morning is cool. One day might find a cheese soufflé with Dijon sauce, sour cream, coffee cake, and fresh berries. The next day could be something totally different.

The inn is on a large corner lot with manicured lawns, flower gardens, and ash, elm, and maple trees. In the warm months the colors of the house are reflected in the old-fashioned flower gardens in front and complemented by the ever changing blues of the distant mountains.

Accommodations: 25 rooms, 23 with private bath. *Driving Instructions:* Take I-25 to exit 143 (Uintah Street), and go east (away from the mountains) three blocks to Cascade Avenue. Turn right on Cascade, and proceed seven blocks to the inn at the corner of Cascade and St. Vrain.

SOWARD RANCH

P.O. Box 130, Creede, CO 81130. 303-658-2295 May 1 to November 1; otherwise 303-658-2228. *Innkeepers:* Margaret and Howard Lamb. Open late May to mid-October.

The Soward Ranch, by the Rio Grande, has been in the same family for a hundred years. Its original section was homesteaded in 1886 by Ellen and Dan Soward, who arrived in the area in 1879 and operated a stagecoach stop and the post office. Margaret Lamb is a granddaughter of the Sowards'. She and her husband, Howard, continue the ranch operation today with their sons Jim, Scott, and Steve, and Steve's wife, Kate.

In 1932, rustic cabins were added over the ranch property; each was assured privacy by its location. The cabins come with full bath, heat, and cooking and refrigeration facilities. Most cabins are fully modernized, but two pioneer cabins are favored by guests who prefer roughing it. Three have fireplaces and one a Franklin stove. At this time the Lambs do not rent horses, offer food, or sell supplies, but it is a pleasant jaunt into Creede for provisions.

Soward Ranch, in a scenic open valley at 9,000 feet and bordered on two sides by national forest, is surrounded by mountains, outstanding views, and fresh air. Trout fishing is the main recreation here, and it is excellent. Mainly, however, Soward Ranch is for relaxing in an unspoiled setting.

Accommodations: 12 housekeeping cabins with private bath. *Pets:* Not permitted. *Driving Instructions:* The ranch is 14 miles southwest of Creede. Drive 7 miles on asphalt road (Route 149), then turn at Middle Creek Road, which has a gravel surface, and continue 7 miles.

Cripple Creek, Colorado

IMPERIAL HOTEL

123 North Third Street, Cripple Creek, CO 80813. 303-689-2713.
Innkeepers: Bonnie and Stephen Mackin. Open mid-May to
mid-October.

The Imperial is the last of the old Cripple Creek hotels to have survived from the boom period before the turn of the century. The hotel
was constructed in 1896. In its heyday it was the queen of the town,
a base for the wining and dining of financiers, geologists, mining engi-
neers, and their clients from the East Coast who assembled in Cripple Creek ready to make their fortunes in the newly discovered gold.
Unlike most mining town hotels built during the boom, the Imperial
never closed its doors except for a brief period during WW II.

When the Mackins bought the three-story hotel in 1946, it was sadly
neglected. Most people in the town felt that the hotel could not be

run as a profitable enterprise, but the Mackins persisted. Room by room they refurbished, installing new furnishings, as well as items rescued from the older Antlers Hotel in Colorado Springs and a back-bar from a local pool hall. The hotel is now a member of the Historic Hotels of the Rocky Mountain/West. The hotel gained a spreading reputation for good food and hospitality. Early on, it made the fortunate decision to invite the Piper Players, a struggling group of actors and actresses, to set up headquarters at the Imperial. The group was signed to present a season of old-time melodramas. The 1948 summer season saw attendance by 4,800, and the theater is now considered to be the foremost exponent of melodrama in the country, presenting only carefully researched plays that are authentic, dating from the 1840-to-1900 period. More than a million people have attended performances. *Time* magazine said of the Imperial Players: "Most melodrama groups are influenced by the quality of the Imperial Players, the 'Old Vic' of modern melodrama." The theater season is from early June through Labor Day.

The Imperial, a classic Victorian hotel, offers thirty guest rooms (plus a modern motel unit). Those wishing a more old-fashioned room furnished with antiques should request one when making their reservations. Guest rooms and public rooms have carefully selected period wallpapers. Many of the furnishings, including the period lighting pieces, have been rescued from historic Colorado buildings slated for demolition. The Mackins saved the front desk and box-office cage from the old First National Bank of Colorado Springs. Stained-glass doors in the dining room as well as leaded and stained-glass panels over the entrance doors were salvaged from the razing of Glockner Hospital and Sanitarium in Colorado Springs. The Red Rooster lounge has a small bar that once served miners in the Red Rooster Saloon near Twin Lakes, Colorado.

The dining rooms at the Imperial serve a luncheon buffet and repeat the buffet in the evening on a more elaborate scale, always featuring roast baron of beef.

Accommodations: 30 rooms, 16 with private bath. *Pets:* Not permitted. *Driving Instructions:* Cripple Creek may be reached by means of Route 67 the year round or by means of the very scenic Gold Camp Road, an improved gravel road, in the summer only.

Denver, Colorado

CAMBRIDGE CLUB

1560 Sherman, Denver, CO 80203. 303-831-1252; toll-free: 800-621-8385 (ext. 917). *Innkeeper:* Jeff Papp. Open all year.

On a quiet tree-lined street in downtown Denver is an elegant small hotel, its 29 suites providing an oasis of old-English warmth in this large contemporary city. The Cambridge Club, built in 1940 and renovated in the 1980s, is just steps away from Denver's financial district, restaurants, and government buildings. Each of the club's suites is individually decorated with English antiques, rich dark woods, original oil paintings, and coordinated fabrics, some forming the canopies on the four-poster beds with matching comforters. Special amenities at the Cambridge Club include limousine service around the city, 24-hour concierge staff, turn-down service with cognac and Swiss chocolate truffles (or milk and cookies if one prefers) placed on the bedside table, and fresh flowers and baskets of fruit in each room. Guests have the use of two athletic clubs in Denver, and the staff will arrange for theater, secretarial services, or a horse-and-buggy tour.

On the garden level, the club's French restaurant, Le Profil, is open Monday through Saturday for lunch and dinner and provides the room service as well. A Continental breakfast is served at bedside. A hospitality suite is open for guests' use until midnight, with a self-service wet bar and coffee and tea.

Accommodations: 29 suites with private bath. *Pets:* Not permitted. *Driving Instructions:* The Club is on Sherman Street between Colfax and 16th streets, 1/2 block from the State Capitol.

Durango, Colorado

BLUE LAKE RANCH

16919 Highway 140, Hesperus, CO 81326. 303-385-4537. *Innkeepers:* David Alford. Open May through September.

Blue Lake Ranch is a genuine working ranch. Jersey cows provide milk, cream, and butter; there are pigs and lambs in the barnyard; and ducks and geese float on the lake. Yet, the ranch also offers elegant, cosmopolitan accommodations, with an eclectic blend of American antiques, Oriental *objets d'art,* plush rugs, and a wide-ranging collection of artwork. Fresh flowers are everywhere—in window boxes, mountain-view guest rooms, the English-style gardens surrounding the patios—and turn-down service, mints on the pillows, an outdoor whirlpool bath, and greenhouse dining are all part of the experience.

The heart of the ranch is a big kitchen with an open hearth and decorative tile-work on counters and floors. Dried herbs and flowers and baskets hang from its rafters, and adjoining it is a comfortable sitting area where tea and pastries are served in the afternoon. The ranch offers breakfasts and dinners to the public—the specialty is ranch-grown lamb seasoned with fresh herbs.

From Blue Lake, one can easily explore nearby Mesa Verde and other Indian ruins as well as the mining towns of Telluride and Silverton.

Accommodations: 4 rooms, 1 with private bath. *Pets and smoking:* Not permitted. *Driving Instructions:* From Durango, drive west on Route 160 to Hesperus. Turn south onto Route 140 and drive 6 2/10 miles to the inn on the right.

GENERAL PALMER HOUSE

567 Main Street, Durango, CO 81301. 303-247-4747; toll-free: 800-523-3358 (outside Colorado). *Innkeeper:* Carolyn Rector. Open all year.

The General Palmer House, built in 1898, was named after General Jackson Palmer, the founder of the Denver and Silverton Narrow Gauge Railroad. The hotel was fully renovated and remodeled in 1986. Today the flavor of the hotel is reminiscent of the earlier era. The lobby and guest rooms are decorated in a Gay Nineties style with Victorian furnishings. The lobby has a solarium and library. The Palace Restaurant, on the first floor of the building's annex, is open to the public for all meals; a Continental breakfast is served to overnight guests. The hotel is adjacent to the narrow-gauge railroad station.

Accommodations: 39 rooms with private bath. *Pets:* Not permitted. *Driving Instructions:* Durango is at the intersection of Routes 550 and 160 in southwestern Colorado. The hotel is on Main Street.

STRATER HOTEL

699 Main Avenue, Durango, Colorado. Mailing address: P.O. Drawer E, Durango, CO 81301. 303-247-4431. *Innkeeper:* Roderick Barker. Open all year.

The Strater is a grand old Victorian hotel. It has been in continuous operation since 1887, when twenty-year-old Henry Strater undertook the task and considerable gamble of building the large luxury hotel in the frontier mining town of Durango. The Strater was leased to a Mr. Rice. After a series of misunderstandings, Mr. Strater spitefully built another hotel, the Columbian, adjoining the original. Eventually both hotels ended up under the ownership of the Barker family, proprietors since 1926. The owner today is Earl A. Barker.

The Strater has been meticulously restored and maintained. Many modern conveniences have been slipped into the Victorian guest rooms, all of which are fully air-conditioned and have phones and television. The rooms have the ornate furniture and decor of the turn of the century, including some of the fanciest walnut high-backed beds to be found anywhere. One features a ceiling-high canopy of carved burled hardwood and a tufted deep-purple velvet lining, accompanying marble-topped dressers, velvet cushioned sofas and chairs, heavy cream-colored bedspreads, and velvet drapes. Ornate gilt frames containing old photographs, prints, and oils decorate the halls and rooms throughout.

The Strater is in the restored historic district of Durango, its sidewalks lit by old gas lanterns. Inside the brick four-story hotel, the lobby, two dining rooms, a saloon, and a 250-seat theater are decked out in Victorian antiques, etched and stained-glass windows, Tiffany-style chandeliers, paintings, and velvets and satins.

The two dining rooms, Henry's and the Columbian Room, offer meals in very different atmospheres. The Columbian Room is formal and dignified, with gold-trimmed mirrors and a large crystal chandelier. The more casual old-time Henry's has Tiffany shades and stained-glass windows. Both dining rooms feature a selection of steaks and a variety of seafoods and pastas.

Diamond Belle Saloon is a popular place, with its honky-tonk piano, and bartenders and cancan girls, all in costume. The Diamond Circle Theater, open in the summer months, presents "turn of the century" plays and vaudeville acts.

Accommodations: 93 rooms with private bath. *Pets:* Only small trained pets are allowed. *Driving Instructions:* Durango is in the far southwest corner of the state, where Route 550, the famous Million Dollar Highway over the mountains, crosses over the Navajo Trail, Route 160, also known as the "Western Wonderway."

Empire, Colorado

Empire is a town of 420 inhabitants a few miles from Georgetown. The region burst into prominence during the gold and silver mining days between 1859 and 1893. When the gold ran out and silver was demonetized, the miners left en masse. But Georgetown survives almost intact, spared of major fires, as a monument to Victorian architecture. Today, most tourists come to the area to enjoy the mountainous terrain, ski at several ski sites, or enjoy the many restored buildings and museums in Georgetown.

THE PECK HOUSE

83 Sunny Avenue, Empire, Colorado. Mailing address: Box 428, Empire, CO 80438. 303-569-9870. *Innkeeper:* Gary and Sally St. Clair. Open all year.

The Peck House is the oldest hotel in Colorado still in operation. Built as the family home of James Peck in 1860, the wood-frame building was initially a four-room house. Peck, a wealthy and adventurous Chicago merchant, was lured west in 1859 by the challenge of the frontier and the chance to find gold. In 1872, he converted his home to the Peck House to accommodate visiting mining executives. Running water was provided by burning lengths of aspen hollow with a hot poker and then fitting them together and running the wooden pipe to a spring to the north of the house. The Peck House had the first electric lights in the area, thanks to power generated by its water wheel. For many years before the automobile, the Peck House was a stop for the stagecoaches running over Berthoud Pass. Over the years, the house was added onto in several directions, and today a long front porch overlooks the valley that first attracted Peck to the area. The present kitchen, bar, and reception area are located within the original building. Much of the furniture dates back to the time of the original owners. Over the years, the Peck House has entertained such luminaries as Generals Grenville Dodge and William Tecumseh Sherman and showman Phineas T. Barnum.

The downstairs portion of the Peck House is primarily devoted to the public rooms. There are two sitting rooms as well as a lounge, a bar, and a dining room. The larger of the sitting rooms has a comfortable arrangement of Victorian furniture including two easy chairs, a pair of rockers, and a bookcase crammed with books available for

guests' reading. This room has the feeling of the front parlor of many homes of the Victorian era. The dining room has red carpeting and white walls on which are hung nineteenth-century prints and photographs of the area. The intimate room has thirteen tables, and a fire frequently burns in its fireplace.

The dining room is open to the public for dinner, Sunday brunch, and Saturday lunch. The dinner menu features a variety of entrées, including steaks, seafoods, and beef and oyster pie from an old-fashioned recipe of Mrs. Peck's. In the summer, lunch is available during the week as well as on weekends.

There are two guest rooms on the ground floor. The Governor's Room is the best in the house, with its chandelier, Eastlake furnishings, and reading corner with a view of the mountains. The Garden Room, on the same floor, has a blend of Western and Victorian antiques with furnishings of bird's-eye maple. A door opens onto the front porch from here. The bridal suite on the second floor is probably the inn's original one. It has views of Union Pass and is furnished in Victorian mahogany.

Accommodations: 11 rooms, 9 with private bath. *Pets:* Not permitted. *Driving Instructions:* Take I-70 to the Empire-Granby exit. The inn is in the center of the town of Empire.

Green Mountain Falls, Colorado

Green Mountain Falls is an alpine village hidden at the foot of Pikes Peak. At an elevation of 7,000 feet in the Ute Pass over the Colorado Rockies, the town was an early stopover for the narrow-gauge gold trains on the Cripple Creek–Colorado Springs run. Green Mountain Falls is quite near popular Colorado Springs with all its tourist attractions.

OUTLOOK LODGE

6975 Howard Road, Green Mountain Falls, Colorado. Mailing address: P.O. Box 5, Green Mountain Falls, CO 80819. 303-684-2303. *Innkeepers:* The Ahern family. Open Memorial Day through Labor Day.

Outlook Lodge is an old "country Victorian" tucked away in the secluded mountain village of Green Mountain Falls at the foot of Pikes Peak. The lodge is a Victorian parsonage built during the Colorado Gold Rush days of the late nineteenth century. In those days the town was a booming tourist mecca with five big hotels on the shores of the stream-fed lake. Outlook Lodge carries on the traditions of warm Western hospitality from the late nineteenth century. The Aherns, while looking for a mountain cabin for family vacations, fell in love with the lodge amid tall pine trees with a little mountain creek running through its property. The building came with stained-glass and big bay windows, spacious dining room, large, comfortable parlor, and most of the original Victorian furnishings. There was even a walk-in pantry. The temptation to buy was irresistible, and the Aherns found themselves running a very popular and successful guest house. The Aherns, freelance writers and teachers, entered wholeheartedly into this new venture.

Lodge rooms are either wood-paneled or papered with floral patterns. Breakfasts are served family-style around the long table in the antique-filled dining room, and a special treat is having a cup of coffee out on the gingerbready veranda overlooking the alpine village of Green Mountain Falls. Freshly baked sweet rolls and carrot, corn, and banana breads come hot from the oven and are served with pots of jams and jellies and fresh creamery butter. The coffee pot is always ready with steaming-hot brew. The parlor is warmed by a tiled fire-

place, and guests are welcome to relax and visit in this room with its plants and old rockers.

The staircase leading to the guest rooms looks like something out of "Goldilocks and the Three Bears"—carved and woodsy. The guest rooms with their spool beds and other period Victorian bedroom furniture blend with the puffy quilts and braided rag rugs to create an atmosphere of old-fashioned comfort.

The lodge is ideally situated one block from the lake, a swimming pool, and the town with its restaurants. There is no lack of entertainment in the area. The town has a stable with horses for hire and tennis courts. Hiking is excellent in the surrounding hills. The Rocky Mountain lakes and streams offer good fishing. Mountain-cool evenings around the lodge's fireplace, a community sing at the old piano, and mornings at the breakfast table with all its muffins and breads make Outlook Lodge the perfect home base for a Colorado vacation. The family atmosphere of this house encourages lasting friendships among guests and their hosts.

Accommodations: 12 rooms, 4 with private bath. *Driving Instructions:* Green Mountain Falls is 15 miles west of Colorado Springs on Route 24.

Hot Sulphur Springs, Colorado

RIVERSIDE HOTEL

509 Grand Avenue, Hot Sulphur Springs, CO 80451. 303-725-3589 or 725-9996. *Innkeeper:* Abraham Renta. Open all year.

Visitors have been attracted to this town ever since the hot springs were discovered. In the early part of this century, trains would stop here daily. Just across the Colorado River from the historic baths, literally at the riverside, is the Riverside Hotel, built in 1903 to accommodate traveling salespersons and visitors to the springs. The building, with breathtaking river and mountain views from the dining room and guest rooms, has always offered simple lodgings, a tradition that continues today. Guest rooms are small and not fancy, but comfortable, fresh, and clean, each with a sink and queen-size iron bed with a print quilt. Hall baths serve the rooms as they have since 1903.

A small pub has an antique back-bar. In cool weather, a fire burns in the lobby hearth. The dining rooms, also with fireplaces and antique furnishings, serve dinner daily to guests and the public all year and lunches in the summer only. There are ski areas nearby.

Accommodations: 20 rooms, 2 with private bath. *Driving Instructions:* From I-70, take the Route 40 exit north to Hot Sulphur Springs.

La Veta, Colorado

1899 INN BED AND BREAKFAST

314 S. Main, La Veta, Colorado. Mailing Address: P.O. Box 372, La Veta, CO 81055. 303-742-3576. *Innkeeper:* Marilyn Hall. Open all year.

This stone building, with its three gables and shady front porch, served as the area hospital until the 1940s, when it was converted to a boarding house. Recently a guest spent his birthday in the very room where he was born back in 1929.

Marilyn Hall has transformed the inn into an informal place furnished with period oak pieces and hooked and braided rugs on dark wood floors. There are fresh bouquets of flowers in the five guest rooms, as well as greenery throughout the inn. The rooms have old-fashioned iron or wooden beds, rocking chairs, and floor-to-ceiling windows. Guests can relax and visit in the living room, warmed by an ornate antique stove known as "Social No. 11." An upright piano and a television hidden behind a door are also in this room.

There is much to keep visitors busy in La Veta. Within 14 miles of the inn are prospecting, mountain climbing, fishing, and excellent downhill and Nordic skiing. La Veta offers breathtaking views of twin peaks that rise 13,000 feet, overlooking Chucara Valley. An added bonus is horseback riding and backpacking excursions with trained outfitters and guides nearby. In summer, there are rodeos, country fairs, and melodramas in La Veta.

Accommodations: 5 rooms, 2 with private bath. *Driving Instructions:* From I-25, exit at Walsenburg and take Route 160 west 11 miles. Turn south on Route 12 and continue five miles to La Veta.

Leadville, Colorado

MOUNTAIN MANSION

129 West 8th Street, Leadville, CO 80461. 303-486-0655. *Inn-keepers:* James and Ana Maria Nezol. Open all year.

Mountain Mansion is the restored estate of an early Colorado governor. It was built in 1892 in this early mining town known locally as "Cloud City." Leadville is 10,500 feet above sea level, yet is dominated by nearby Mount Massive at 14,421 feet. Ana Maria Nezol offers overnight guests a chance to sample Argentinian and Venezuelan breakfasts. The inn features Victorian suites decorated with velvet and lace. Each of the three suites has a fireplace. In addition to the suites, there are humbler, more functional guest rooms, with cooking facilities, as well as a European hostel-style room for budget-minded travelers. Guests are incorporated into the family at breakfast and again in the evening, when townspeople join guests and the innkeepers for fireside history lessons, readings, singalongs, and musical get-togethers. There is a warm, informal atmosphere enhanced by flowers and crackling fires.

Accommodations: 7 rooms, 3 with private bath. *Driving Instructions:* Take I-70 to the Copper Mountain/Leadville exit. Continue on Colorado Route 91 into Leadville. At the first light, turn left. Take the first right onto West 8 Street.

GRAY'S AVENUE HOTEL

711 Manitou Avenue, Manitou Springs, CO 80829. 303-685-1277. *Innkeepers:* Tom and Lee Gray. Open all year except mid-December through January.

Manitou Springs is a historic preservation district. The carbonated mineral springs were considered sacred by the Native Americans. Later, the healing waters attracted travelers, creating a need for lodgings. The Avenue Hotel, built in 1880, was one such place.

The three-story Queen Anne Victorian was restored by Lee and Tom Gray. It is next to a large park, giving it a country air. The inn's foyer is flanked by a formal Victorian parlor, the dining room, and a family room with a television set and a video-cassette recorder by the fireside. One of the ten guest rooms is a three-room suite with a sitting room. Another, The General's Room, overlooks the grounds of the Library. The Dragon Room is a sunny rear room done in natural woods. Country-style breakfasts are served in the dining room, and several restaurants are nearby.

Accommodations: 10 rooms, 3 with private bath. *Pets:* Not permitted. *Children:* Under 10 not permitted. *Driving Instructions:* From I-25, take Highway 24 west 4.4 miles to the Manitou Avenue exit. Continue west for 1.1 miles. The inn is on the left.

Norwood, Colorado

BACK NARROWS INN

Route 145, Norwood, CO 81423. 303-327-4417. *Innkeepers:* Terre and Joyce Bucknam. Open all year.

Just getting to the Back Narrows Inn is a treat. Route 141 heads northwest through the steep, red-walled Uniweep Canyon, whereas Route 62, from the east, climbs the Dallas Divide, offering spectacular vistas of the Sneffels Mountain Range. Back Narrows Inn has been welcoming travelers to Norwood since 1883. The town is at the edge of the San Juan Mountains, 33 miles from Telluride.

Joyce and Terre Bucknam bought the inn in the early 1970s, and a whole lot of elbow grease and enthusiasm have gone into its restoration since. Layers of paint were stripped away, revealing oak paneling beneath. Old linoleum was discarded, and hardwood floors were covered with bright carpets. Country antiques decorate each room, and old trunks serve as bedside tables in the guest rooms. The lobby–sitting room has baskets of pine cones and dried bouquets of wild grasses and cattails set around. A television set and a potbellied stove invite get-togethers with other guests and local residents. The inn's bar and restaurant are open Thursday through Sunday. Terre is known as "The Colorado Bookman," and his bookshop of old and rare books is fun to browse in.

There are recreational activities in the area, including cross-country skiing in the national forest and downhill skiing at Telluride.

Accommodations: 10 rooms, several with private baths. *Driving Instructions:* From Telluride take Route 145 northwest to Norwood and the inn. Route 145 can be reached via Route 141 or 62.

Ouray, Colorado

BAKER'S MANOR GUEST HOUSE

317 Second Street, Ouray, CO 81427. 303-325-4574. *Innkeepers:* Gem Mahan and Ivan Rudd. Open all year.

Ouray is a valley village surrounded by the San Juan mountains. Baker's Manor is a pleasant alternative to the area motels as a base to enjoy a region that (like many others in the Rockies) has dubbed itself the "Switzerland of America." As you enter the canyon from the surrounding mountains, you will certainly agree that the Ouray region is a top contender for the title. At an altitude of 7,800 feet, Baker's Manor is one of the loftiest inns we have listed. The Victorian house, built in 1881, offers guest rooms that are furnished with antiques and have striking views of the area. To start the day, complimentary juice, fruit, rolls, and coffee are served.

Accommodations: 6 rooms sharing a bath and separate shower. *Pets:* Not permitted. *Driving Instructions:* Take U.S. 550 to the center of Ouray. The guest house is one block west of Main Street between Third and Fourth avenues.

ST. ELMO HOTEL

426 Main Street, Ouray, Colorado. Mailing address: P.O. Box 667, Ouray, CO 81427. 303-325-4951. *Innkeepers:* Sandy and Dan Lingenfelter. Open all year.

In 1898, Mrs. Kitty Heit built the Hotel St. Elmo to augment her successful Bon-Ton restaurant. The hotel has been in continuous operation ever since, first serving miners, then the travelers who slowly became a source of income to the town as the mining efforts declined. The St. Elmo is a sturdy brick two-story building heavily influenced by the art nouveau style rather than the strictly Victorian movement popular at the time. The hotel has a large, old-fashioned lobby frequented by guests who gather there for coffee or tea. Most of the original furnishings have survived, an advantage peculiar to hotels that have remained in continuous use. Two of the best guest accommodations are the Presidential Suite and the Honeymoon Suite, with its antique half-tester bed.

The Bon-Ton Restaurant lives on at the St. Elmo, though it offers a different menu from Kitty's days. It is Italian in derivation, except for the steak items and fresh (daily) seafood. A breakfast of freshly baked breads and muffins and fresh fruit is served.

Ouray is known as the "Jeep Capital of the World" because of the hundreds of miles of trails in the high country, which wind through ghost towns and mountain meadows, past waterfalls and 13,000-foot peaks.

Accommodations: 11 rooms, 7 with private bath. *Pets:* Not permitted. *Driving Instructions:* Take Route 550 to the center of Ouray and the hotel.

Redstone, Colorado

THE HISTORIC REDSTONE INN

    0082 Redstone Boulevard, Redstone, CO 81623. 303-963-2526.
Open all year.

The Historic Redstone Inn was constructed by industrialist and coal baron John Cleveland Osgood in 1902. Osgood needed housing for his bachelor miners and for the many guests he attracted to the area but did not wish to entertain at his neighboring Cleveholm Manor. The inn, a copy of a Dutch tavern, has a clock tower rising from one corner of the U-shaped three-story half-timbered building. Another distinctive feature is the balconies that surround each floor. The latest addition to the inn was provided by Frank Kistler of the Hotel Colorado, who bought the inn in the 1950s and added a wing in 1956. This wing has Western-style rooms, each with two double beds and more contemporary furnishings. All but four open onto the second-floor balcony, with views of the town of Redstone and the surrounding mountains. The rooms in the older section have many original antiques, including some of the hand-pegged miner's furniture. The third-floor guest rooms are a bargain although all share a hall bath.

A major restoration project closed the Historic Redstone Inn for a year. The rooms were remodeled, and modern conveniences including telephones, television, and private baths were fitted into the old-fashioned inn. The public rooms include a dining room with a fireplace and two parlors, also with fireplaces. Throughout the inn are collections of antique paintings, tapestries, and furniture. The inn has a distinctly European atmosphere enhanced by its rural mountain setting. Its restaurant is open to the public for breakfast, lunch, and dinner, as well as Sunday brunch.

In summer the inn offers a tennis court and horseback-riding stables on its grounds. The Crystal River flows past the lawns and tall trees, offering soothing sounds and good fishing as well. In winter cross-country skiers may use the trails at the inn. Sleigh rides through the winter landscape are favorites with guests.

Accommodations: 35 rooms, 31 with private bath. *Pets:* Not permitted. *Driving Instructions:* From Route 82 take Route 133 south. The inn is on Redstone Boulevard, just off Route 133.

Silverton is one of the few mining towns that refused to die. In the San Juan Mountains of Colorado, the town grew to mining prominence following the completion of the narrow-gauge railroad from Durango. Town notables included Bat Masterson, imported for his law-enforcing skills during the wild and woolly days before the turn of the century. Many of the original buildings from that period are preserved on Blair Street in the town.

GRAND IMPERIAL HOTEL

1219 Greene Street, Silverton, Colorado. Mailing address: P.O. Box 97, Silverton, CO 81433. 303-387-5527. *Innkeepers:* Mary Helen and Ken Marlin. Open March through September.

The Grand Imperial is a brick-and-stone Victorian hotel built in 1882 by an Englishman to serve the newly opened narrow-gauge railroad. The Denver and Rio Grande Railroad connected the many mines of Silverton with the smelters at Durango. Today, the line is run as a tourist attraction. Stones for the sides of the hotel were gathered locally, and the bricks were made especially at local brick kilns. Plans for this hotel were made well in advance of its actual construction. The best witness to this is the cherry back bar that survives today in the lounge. It is more than 35 feet long and was constructed especially for the Grand Imperial in 1879, three years before the hotel opened its doors. It was then shipped around Cape Horn to San Francisco, where it was put on several covered wagons and sent over the rugged trails to Silverton. It has stood in the same spot for about a century.

The hotel has undergone large-scale restoration. Care has been taken to maintain the Victorian atmosphere throughout the hotel. The guest rooms are mostly decorated with period antiques that include brass and iron beds and accessory pieces from the same period. The lobby has a second bar that was recently installed as a showpiece, having spent many decades in a variety of taverns throughout Silverton. A distinctive feature of the dining room is its black walnut tables, unique in the locale. There are several mementos of past gambling at the Grand Imperial, including a handsome antique roulette table. The innkeeper is proud of a sailing ship carved by Joseph Imhoff around the turn of the century and given to the hotel in its youth. Imhoff was

a noted painter as well as a wood-carver; his portait of Lillian Russell hangs in the lobby.

The dining room at the Grand Imperial serves a selection of American cooking with the emphasis on simple fare of the meat-and-potatoes variety. There are steaks, chops, trout, roasts, and shrimp dishes—all accompanied by home-baked breads, rolls, and pastries. The lounge features live entertainment daily in summer and on special weekends in winter. This area is an excellent spot for all kinds of winter sports, and the Grand Imperial offers skiers packages for the Purgatory Ski Area nearby.

Accommodations: 40 rooms with private bath. *Pets:* Not permitted. *Driving Instructions:* Route 550 runs directly into Silverton and becomes Greene Street.

Dizzy Gillespie is quoted as saying: "If Telluride ain't paradise, then heaven can wait." Whatever Telluride is, it certainly is having a renaissance following many years of financial depression that ensued after billions of dollars in precious minerals were wrenched from its many miles of mining tunnels. Telluride's new mother lode is the skiing boom. Surrounded by the 14,000-foot peaks of the San Juan mountains, the Telluride Ski Area dominates the local downhill action. The Plunge is the steepest and one of the longest ski runs in North America, descending over a vertical drop of 3,200 feet. The town is filled with historic buildings.

JOHNSTONE INN

403 West Colorado Avenue, Telluride, Colorado. Mailing address: Box 546, Telluride, CO 81435. 303-728-3316. *Innkeepers:* Christine and Michael Courter. Open all year except April and early November.

The Johnstone Inn is a little Victorian bed-and-breakfast place at the edge of the resort village of Telluride. Visitors are welcomed by a veranda and a flight of stairs sporting grape-colored railings and balustrades. Built in 1893 and restored in 1978, the inn has many of its original accoutrements such as old-fashioned lighting fixtures, dark woodwork, and even an old tin bathtub. A purple-and-violet stained-glass window softly lights the hall landing. The inn is furnished with Victorian antiques and more recently made pieces.

When the Continental breakfast, the only meal available, is served in the dining room, the aroma of freshly baked nut bread fills the air. The inn is just three blocks from the Coonskin Lift, and shuttle service to the lift is available in front of the house.

Telluride is a Mecca for Alpine and Nordic skiing but should not be missed in warmer seasons as well. The surrounding mountains offer superb hiking, jeep riding, and fishing, and many local festivals are held in summer.

Accommodations: 8 rooms, 1 with private bath. *Pets:* Not permitted. *Driving Instructions:* Telluride is on Route 145 in southwestern Colorado.

NEW SHERIDAN HOTEL AND BAR

231 West Colorado Avenue, Telluride, Colorado. Mailing address: P.O. Box 980, Telluride, CO 81435. 303-728-4351. *Innkeeper:* Wendy McFadden. Open all year.

The New Sheridan, a three-story brick hotel, was built in 1895 and 1899. The handsome Victorian structure was the pride of Telluride in its youth and offered, for many years, the finest food and lodging in the area. As the mining era that had caused Telluride to flourish at the turn of the century began to wane, so did the fortunes of the New Sheridan. Then, in 1977, an Ohio developer and renovator of historic buildings, Walter C. McClellan, bought the old building.

Today, the New Sheridan is a fully modern hotel that has been restored and renovated to retain its Victorian ambience while incorporating such modern conveniences as private bathrooms. Each of its bedrooms has brass beds, oak furniture, and stained-glass lighting fixtures. On the first floor is an authentic Victorian bar and lounge, the centerpiece of which is the long cherrywood bar that was imported for the New Sheridan from Austria when the hotel opened in the 1890s. The bar was used in several scenes of a 20th Century-Fox movie about Butch Cassidy and the Sundance Kid. The bar's rear wall is a stained-glass partition that separates the bar from a smaller room often used for backgammon. Also on this floor is a northern-Italian restaurant, Julian's, which serves a variety of dishes from traditional pastas to oysters Genovese and chicken Amafitano. Outside the hotel is a landscaped patio called the Sheridan Garden, which is used for lunch and cocktails during the summer months.

Accommodations: 21 rooms, 9 with private bath; 1 suite. *Pets:* Not permitted. *Driving Instructions:* Take Colorado 145 directly into Telluride.

Idaho

INDIAN CREEK GUEST RANCH

Route 2, Box 105, North Fork, ID 83466. *Telephone:* Dial area code 208 operator, and ask for the Salmon, Idaho, operator. Ask for 24F 211 (a ring-down phone number). *Innkeepers:* Jack and Lois Briggs. Open May through October.

Indian Creek offers truly remote, rustic vacationing. The ranch consists of a main lodge and four guests cabins scattered on the property, which is ringed by rough stone walls. Mountain slopes rise abruptly from behind the cabins, and the smell of a pine fire in the fireplace greets you on arrival. If you are heading to Indian Creek, plan to put behind you your dependence on some of the refinements of civilization. There is no electricity here, only propane-powered gas lamps. However, each cabin has its own hot and cold running water and private bathroom. The lone radio-telephone in the lodge is run by battery power, so don't plan to conduct long-distance business conference from the ranch.

The main lodge was known as the Red Onion Bar in the 1890s and early twentieth century, when the stagecoach went through the property and on out to Ulysses, now a ghost town. The lodge borders on the Idaho wilderness and has a screened-in dining room looking out over the mountains. It serves simple, family-style meals such as prime ribs, steaks, chicken, spaghetti, barbecued ribs, hot rolls, biscuits, and muffins. The fishing for trout is good in the stream, and the Briggses will be happy to cook up your catch the same day for dinner.

The guest rooms have peeled log walls and braided rugs. One has a fireplace and a window wall that seems to bring scenery inside. Most guests (never more than ten at a time) come to put city life behind them and rest; but the ranch offers a number of activities including a

variety of trail rides through the neighboring mountains. Guests can arrange for one-day float trips on the Salmon River (known locally and alarmingly as the "River of No Return") as well as trips to the Gold Rush ghost town of Ulysses. There are jeep trips into the surrounding wilderness, and trips to fishing holes along the nearby river. The riding, jeep trips, guide, and meals are included in the American-plan rates quoted in the chart-index at the end of this volume. Indian Creek is a relaxing place where you are made to feel at home in the mountains by people who live there.

Accommodations: 4 cabins with private bath. *Driving Instructions:* The ranch is 12 miles downstream from North Fork, Idaho. Get specific instructions when making reservations. The ranch will pick guests up at the airport or in Salmon.

GRANDVIEW LODGE AND RESORT

Priest Lake, Idaho. Mailing address: Star Route Box 48, Reeder Bay, Priest Lake, ID 83848. 208-443-2433. *Innkeepers:* Bob and Dorothy Benscoter. Open all year.

Grandview Lodge and Resort is on Priest Lake in the Kaniksu National Forest of northern Idaho. The resort began with a few cabins in 1936. In 1965 a log cabin–style modern lodge with wide sun decks was built right out over the water. The lodge has its own marina, dock, and long stretch of beach. Large picture windows in the lodge face the south end of the lake with panoramic views of 12 miles of blue lake, a pine forested shore, islands, and the snow-capped peaks of the northern Idaho mountains. The upper level of the lodge has guest rooms opening onto the sundecks overlooking the lake; other guest rooms are in the north wing, and all are furnished in a modern decor. Guest accommodations are also found in the cabins and condominium-like units with kitchens, bedrooms, baths, wood-burning fireplaces, and decks and porches overlooking the lawns and lakefront area.

In the lower level of the lodge, guests will find a cocktail lounge with a big fireplace. A window-walled dining room is just off the lounge, and both rooms have fine views of the wilderness lake and mountains. The lounge and dining room are open to guests and the public for all meals. The Grandview is a real resort with most of the resort trappings: dancing in the lounge, a heated outdoor swimming pool, and full marine facilities (canoe, boat, and motor rentals). In the summer guests can water ski, swim, hike, fish, and boat around the 26-mile-long lake and its many secluded islands. Canoe float trips and horseback riding are available in the area. The entire area is sparsely populated and offers the serenity of wilderness unmarked by roads and other signs of civilization.

Accommodations: 8 lodge rooms with private bath; 20 cottages. *Pets:* Not permitted. *Driving Instructions:* From Priest River go north on Route 57 for 36 miles to Reeder Bay Road. Then go east for 3 1/2 miles on Reeder Bay Road to the lodge.

Montana

VOSS INN BED AND BREAKFAST

319 South Willson, Bozeman, MT 59715. 406-587-0982. *Innkeepers:* Ruthmary and Ken Tonn. Open all year.

The town of Bozeman is in the Gallatin Valley, not far from Yellowstone National Park and Big Sky, Montana. Voss Inn is one of many Victorian homes that dot the town, facing a tree-lined street not far from Montana State University. It was built in 1883 by Matt Alderson for his bride who died in childbirth two years later. The house was then sold to a retired Civil War colonel, O. P. Chisholm, who doubled its size, creating a ballroom and a billiard room for entertaining, something the Chisholms did lavishly for over 20 years.

Ruthmary and Kenn Tonn have handsomely restored and decorated their inn. The polished wood floors, woodwork, and richly hued wallpapers set off the antiques, oriental rugs, and decorative items from the Victorian period. The parlor is home to an upright piano, a Victrola, and color television, in addition to books and board games.

The guest rooms are decorated with dark, bold wallpapers, ornate brass and painted iron beds, stained-glass lamps, and silk flowers. Full breakfasts are served in the guest rooms, and guests can help themselves to fresh rolls from the fanciful bunwarmer in the hall.

Accommodations: 6 rooms with private bath. *Pets:* Not permitted. *Driving Instructions:* Take the Bozeman exit from I-90. From Main Street, turn south onto Willson and drive 4 blocks to the inn.

Essex, Montana

IZAAK WALTON INN

P.O. Box 653, Essex, MT 59916. 406-888-5700. *Innkeepers:* Larry and Lynda Vielleux. Open all year.

The Izaak Walton is a railroad hotel built in 1939 by the Great Northern Railway, which developed much of the area around and in Glacier National Park. The three-story, half-timbered building was restored in 1974 and again in 1982 by its latest owners. The result is a hotel that harks back to the days when the only access to this area was behind steam locomotives that chugged over trestles and through tunnels in the mountains. The railway operations continue to be an attraction for many guests, who enjoy watching the helper engines push the trains on their way to Marias Pass. The innkeepers will gladly steer their guests to the best vantage points for photographing the helper operation, as well as the scenic trestles, overpasses, snow sheds, and tunnels. Amtrak stops in Essex.

The pine-paneled guest rooms on the top two floors have changed little since the hotel first opened. The original furniture is still in place in the rooms, each of which has a double and a single bed, a dresser, and two chairs. The rooms also have sinks and a tiny night table. Many have Stu Cassidy wildlife pictures on the walls. Nine deluxe rooms have private bathrooms with shower and toilet.

On the first floor are the lounge, lobby, and dining room. The lobby now contains the post office for the tiny town of Essex. There are currently only twenty-five boxes in use. Railroad prints adorn many of the inn's walls, including those of the basement bar and game room. Other railroad memorabilia and pieces of early equipment hang there for buffs to enjoy.

A sauna and a laundromat are available at the inn, and three meals are served daily to guests and the public. A standard menu is offered in the dining room, as well as daily specials such as sage-stuffed pork chops and beef au jus. Hot apple pie à la mode is a house specialty.

The inn is a natural base for many types of outdoor recreation. In summer there is hiking on nearby trails in the Great Bear Wilderness area (more than 1,000 miles of trails) and in the Bob Marshall Wilderness. Fishermen can walk to the Middle Fork River or hike to Marion Lake. There are many streams and lakes within easy driving distance in the surrounding wilderness and Glacier National Park. In the winter the inn is a major ski-touring center. It has doorstep access to miles of maintained cross-country ski trails. Skis and equipment are available for rental at the fully equipped ski shop.

The Izaak Walton is a remote railroad inn set against the backdrop of some of the best mountain scenery in the Rockies. The accommodations are not as luxurious as at many inns on the East or West Coast, but the setting and the congeniality of the innkeepers easily make up for that.

Accommodations: 30 rooms, 9 with private bath. *Pets:* Not permitted. *Driving Instructions:* The hotel is 1/4 mile from Route 2 between East Glacier and West Glacier, at the southern end of Glacier National Park. The only sign is the one for Essex, and it is easy to miss. Essex is also accessible via Amtrak.

Glacier National Park, Montana

Glacier National Park, in the far northwestern part of Montana, was named for its sixty extant glaciers. It has, in addition, snow-crested peaks, waterfalls, and green forests. There are a thousand miles of trout streams, more than two hundred lakes, and an abundance of wildlife that includes deer, elk, mountain goat, and bear. The park is contiguous with *Waterton Lakes National Park* across the Canadian border, making this a truly international park area.

A worthwhile introduction to Glacier National Park is the 50-mile drive along Going-to-the-Sun Road that runs from Saint Mary on the east side of the park to Apgar on the southwest side. This is one of the most scenic roads in the world. Driven from west to east, it skirts mountain-rimmed Lake McDonald, rises into the high country along the Garden Wall, crosses Logan Pass above timberline, and descends toward Saint Mary Lake. While safe and well designed, it is narrow and winding as it ascends the Garden Wall toward the pass. Vehicles wider than 8 feet—including mirrors and other extensions—or longer than 30 feet overall are prohibited on the road between Avalanche

Creek and the *Rising Sun Campgrounds* during July and August. Before July 1 and after August 31, an overall length of 35 feet is permitted.

GLACIER PARK LODGE

East Glacier Park, MT 59434. Winter mailing address: Glacier Park, Inc., Greyhound Tower–Mail Station 5510, Phoenix, AZ 85077. 406-226-5551; 602-248-6000 in winter. Open early June through mid-September.

Glacier Park Lodge is considered by Glacier Park, Inc., to be "the Company's premier hotel." With the mountains forming a backdrop, you can swim in a heated pool, ride horseback across the valley, fish in glacier-fed lakes, relax in manicured annual and perennial gardens, or play golf on a 3,350-yard nine-hole course.

As at the Lake MacDonald Lodge and the Many Glacier Hotel in this park, it is the cavernous lobby that sets the tone for the entire building. As you leave the gardens and enter the hotel, you are immediately struck by the size of the Douglas firs used in the lobby. The Great Northern Railway, builder of the hotel in 1912–14, shipped them from the Pacific Northwest on flatcars. Sixty trees still covered with their original bark and standing 40 feet in height, with an average diameter of 40 inches, serve as pillars.

The extraordinary design for the building resulted from collaboration between S. L. Bartlett and Thomas D. McMahon, two Chicago architects. McMahon went on to design the Many Glacier Hotel after completing work on Glacier Park Lodge. The guest rooms at this lodge have painted plaster walls and hardwood floors with throw rugs. About half face the mountains, and the remainder face the gardens. Most have balconies, except for those on the third floor.

Accommodations: 155 rooms with private bath. *Pets:* Permitted if leashed. *Driving Instructions:* Take I-2 or Route 49 to East Glacier. The hotel is near the park's eastern entrance near East Glacier.

MANY GLACIER HOTEL

Glacier National Park, Montana. Winter mailing address: Glacier Park, Inc., Greyhound Tower–Mail Station 5510, Phoenix, AZ 85077. 406-226-5551; 602-248-6000 in winter. Open early June through mid-September.

The Many Glacier Hotel, with 209 rooms, is the largest hostelry owned and operated by the Glacier Park, Inc. At the foot of Swiftcurrent Lake and the Swiftcurrent Valley, the hotel is a good base for exploring the park in general and for other nearby activities such as hiking, horseback riding, trout fishing, and canoeing. Launch rides and horseback treks depart from the hotel grounds.

More than four hundred men were employed in the construction of the hotel over a two-year period in 1914 and 1915. Like most of the early park buildings, the Many Glacier Hotel was a project of the Great Northern Railway, which fostered national interest in tourism in the Wyoming and Montana area. The lumber to build the hotel was all felled and milled in the Swiftcurrent Valley. Designed by the Chicago architect Thomas McMahon, the hotel was built at a cost of $500,000. Roads to the site had to be constructed, a sawmill had to be built, and a quarry had to be developed just to handle the materials for the structure.

The lobby is the hotel's focal point, with a dozen or so logs at its perimeter supporting the three-story-high cathedral ceiling. In the center of the lobby is a free-standing fireplace with seats around it on all four sides. One entire wall of the lobby is windows, offering a view of Swiftcurrent Lake. An outdoor balcony gives guests an additional spot from which to enjoy the view. Because of the Alpine appearance of the hotel and its location in the center of what Theodore Roosevelt called the American Alps, it carries out a Swiss theme in much of its decor. The Swiss white cross on a red background and Swiss crest are emblazoned on every guest-room door. For many years, the hotel has hired a student staff whose members combine service skills with an interest in the fine arts, particularly music and drama. Often guests have the opportunity to hear their waiters and waitresses perform choral works during the evening.

Numerous guest rooms at the Many Glacier Hotel face the lake and have doors to their own wooden balconies. Most guest rooms have hardwood floors, although some have been carpeted. The rooms' atmosphere is rustic and comfortable with beamed ceilings and either painted-plaster or paneled walls. The furniture is largely heavy oak, but almost all of the original furnishings have been replaced in the more than seventy years since the hotel opened.

The dining-room menu changes throughout the season and from year to year.

Accommodations: 209 rooms with private bath. *Pets:* Permitted on a leash in the hotel but not on trails in the park. *Driving Instructions:* The most direct access to the hotel is via the paved road from Babb, on the eastern border of the park. Take Route 89 to Babb.

Nevada

THE WINGFIELD HOUSE

219 Court Street, Reno, NV 89501. 702-348-0766. *Innkeepers:* David and Jana Ketchum. Open all year except the first two weeks of February.

Wingfield House is in the center of the older section of Reno on the Truckee River. The 27-room mansion was built in 1907 and, today, welcomes vacationers and businesspeople alike. It occupies a block-long lot in the heart of Reno, surrounded by trees and lawns. There are two large parlors with formal Victorian furnishings and working hearths. A sun room adjoins the dining room, where guests are served a full breakfast on white linen cloths, complete with candlelight and light classical music.

Each guest room has its own special quality. Prince George Room has a fireplace and looks out over the landscaped private grounds and the river. The French Garden Room is romantic, and Cook's bedroom has a porch and a private entrance. The inn provides a base for exploring the area and the casinos, just three blocks away.

Accommodations: 5 rooms with private bath. *Pets:* Not permitted. *Children:* Under 12 not permitted. *Driving Instructions:* The inn is two blocks west of the intersection of Virginia and Court streets.

MIZPAH HOTEL AND CASINO

100 Main Street, Tonopah, Nevada. Mailing address: P.O. Box 952, Tonopah, NV 89049. 702-482-6202. *Innkeeper:* William Allison. Open all year.

The Mizpah is billed as "an elegant retreat into Nevada's past." In 1900, Belle and Jim Butler staked out their claims on a rich vein of silver and gold, reviving a depressed Nevada and sparking a new boom in the mining. Seven years later, the Mizpah Hotel had its gala grand opening, boasting such amenities as hot and cold water, gas and electric service (all previously unheard of here), carpets of the "finest Brussels quality," and a grill room with "shiny new silverware and new crockery ... to fulfill the wants of Tonopah people." Over the years, the hotel has been host to many notables. Tonopah's local hero, Jack Dempsey, went on to become a champion boxer, but not before working as a bouncer-bartender at the Mizpah.

In 1976, the Scott Corporation, owners of Las Vegas's Union Plaza Hotel, took over the Mizpah and began a total restoration and renovation. Spacious, elegant elevator lobbies were opened up on each of the five floors, and period Victorian antiques were brought in. The claw-footed tubs were reporcelained, and the original commodes with their oak water boxes and brass pull chains were reconditioned. Throughout the hotel, the solid oak doors and mahogany trim were stripped and cleaned, and brass beds were polished until they gleamed. Appearance and atmosphere transport guests back to Tonopah's boom-town days but there are such modern additions in the rooms as color television, radios, and individual climate control.

Employees are dressed in uniforms of the 1900s, and period entertainment is featured in the main casino. Two restaurants are open to guests and the public. The hotel's Key Pittman Room, open twenty-four hours a day, serves a menu of traditional American fare from omelets to steaks. The Jack Dempsey Room offers a Continental menu. The casino area has many antiques from the town's colorful past. Two beautiful vault doors are displayed, as is a lantern from the first train to Reno.

Accommodations: 54 rooms with private bath. *Pets:* Not permitted. *Driving Instructions:* The Mizpah Hotel is halfway between Las Vegas and Reno, Nevada, on U.S. 95.

OLD PIONEER GARDEN

Unionville, Nevada. Mailing address: Star Route Unionville 79, Imlay, NV 89418. 702-538-7585. *Innkeepers:* Mitzi and Lew Jones. Open all year.

Mark Twain mentioned his visits to the Old Pioneer Garden in *Roughing It.* Among the historic cottages and buildings on the property is Bonnifield House, with its fieldstone walls, where Twain dined several times. At an elevation of 5,000 feet, there are sweeping views of the stark Buena Vista Valley and the Humboldt Mountains, an area that appears nearly unchanged from pioneer times.

The main farmhouse features gardens and a gazebo alongside a mountain stream, where in warm weather guests may enjoy breakfast. Guest accommodations are in Ross House, a small old-fashioned cabin in a wooded grove; Hadley House, with its library; Bonnifield House; and the main house. The Old Pioneer Garden is encircled with a woven willow fence designed to keep the deer out and the innkeepers' goats in. There is also a fish-catching dog and a number of other farm animals, along with miles of bridle trails for cross-prairie riding and a fully equipped kitchen for guests' use.

Accommodations: 11 rooms, 3 with private bath. *Driving Instructions:* From Winnemucca, take I-80 west 28 miles to Route 400. Drive south 16 miles, turn right, and drive 3 miles to Unionville.

Virginia City, Nevada

Between Carson City and Reno on the far western edge of the state, historic Virginia City flourished as a mining town in the mid-nineteenth century. It was known as the Queen of the Comstock Lode, and its mines produced nearly a billion dollars in gold and silver, helping to finance the building of San Francisco and the Union Army in the Civil War. The town is a popular tourist attraction, visited by half a million people anually. The silver kings built fabulous mansions and saloons; these marvels and the old mines, *Chinatown,* and the *Piper's Opera House* stood virtually untouched from the mines' closings in the early twentieth century through World War II. After the war the town began its comeback and is now a flourishing, elegant restoration town. Private owners have painstakingly restored the Victorian homes and mansions. The Piper's Opera House, the mansions, and saloons are open to visitors. There are mine tours, and in summer the *V & T Railroad* is a popular tourist ride. Virtually every building in this town is of historic significance. The town provides visitors with guided tours and maps of the area.

SAVAGE MANSION

146 South D Street, Virginia City, Nevada. Mailing address: P.O. Box 445, Virginia City, NV 89440. 702-847-0574. *Innkeepers:* Bob and Irene Kugler and Ann Louise Mertz. Open all year.

In 1879, former President Ulysses S. Grant came to Virginia City especially to thank the miners there for the millions of dollars of gold and silver that they had wrenched from the hillsides surrounding the city. Grant and his wife toured the mines and were feted in grand style, including an elaborate roast beef dinner at the Savage Mansion. They remained at the mansion for two nights in the room that is now called the Grant Room, one of those available to overnight guests in this restored Victorian home. Even as Grant spoke, Virginia City was on the verge of decline. Fire had destroyed portions of the town four years earlier, and the mines would no longer be as highly productive. In the ensuing years, time would take its toll on the Savage Mansion, and it would sink almost to ruin before being saved by the restoration efforts of the current owners.

The mansion was built in 1861 as the home of the superintendent of the Savage Mine. He maintained his living quarters on the top two

floors, with the lower floor devoted to the business of the company and serving as its assay office. Set into the hillside, the mansion has a fine Mansard roof ringed with a series of dormers and shows detailing on its street-level fence and on the balustrade of the upstairs balcony. The current owners have proceeded room by room to restore the Victorian elegance of the Gold Rush era. All furnishings are in period style, including many of the original pieces that graced the superintendent's home, including the beds in the guest rooms. The shared bathroom features the original copper bathtub and a functioning 1890 toilet. (The 1878 original is on display in the mansion.) The period carpeting and wall coverings carry through the Victorian theme. Two parlors are for use by guests, some of whom frequently play the 1892 organ. Breakfast, served in the Victorian kitchen, is the only meal available.

Accommodations: 6 rooms, 1 with private bath. *Pets:* Not permitted. *Children:* Discouraged. *Driving Instructions:* Virginia City is reached by taking Route 17.

New Mexico

LA POSADA DE CHIMAYO

Box 463, Chimayó, NM 87522. 505-351-4605. *Innkeeper:* Sue Far-rington. Open all year.

Chimayó is one of many interesting rural villages along the High Road (Routes 4, 520, and 76) to Taos. It is famous for its fine tradition of Spanish weaving, and its shops offer excellent weavings at reasonable prices. The Santuario Church in Chimayó is famous for its curative "mud" and for its Good Friday pilgrimage.

La Posada de Chimayó is a recently constructed guest house that was built using traditional regional building techniques. The two-unit structure has brick floors, *vigas* (roof beams), herringbone ceilings, Mexican tilework, corner fireplaces, and typical of the region, an extensive use of adobe. In one area, tradition has given way to solar ingenuity. A Trombé wall of adobe absorbs heat by day to provide warmth during the winter months. Most furnishings and rugs in the guest rooms are of Mexican origin, and the beds are covered with handmade quilts. "Posada" means resting place, and La Posada de Chimayó is just that—a place where the smell of piñon-pine smoke and the crowing of roosters have replaced the sounds and smells of urban life.

Other than breakfast, no meals are served at La Posada. However, the Rancho de Chimayó in town is one of the region's finest Mexican restaurants. Operated within the ancestral home of its owner, Arturo Jaramillo, it is the reason many visitors first come to Chimayó.

Accommodations: 2 rooms with private bath. *Pets:* Inquire first. *Driving Instructions:* Take New Mexico Route 76 into Chimayó and turn north opposite the Manzana Center. The guest house is about 1 mile from the highway.

Cloudcroft, New Mexico

THE LODGE

U.S. 82, Cloudcroft, New Mexico. *Mailing address:* Box 497, Cloudcroft, NM 88317. 505-682-2566. *Innkeepers:* Glynda and Ted Bonnell. Open all year.

The original Lodge, constructed on a summit near the Alamogordo and Sacramento Mountain Railway, which owned and operated it, was destroyed by fire in 1909. The Lodge was rebuilt on a more scenic site and has been in continuous operation ever since. Once owned by Conrad Hilton, The Lodge has been host to many important visitors, including every New Mexico governor and several presidents and astronauts.

The Lodge, a full-scale mountain resort, is dominated by a central tower where guests frequently gather to watch the spectacular mountain sunsets and for the view encompassing 160 miles of mountains, forests, and the White Sands Proving Ground. The lobby has a fireplace, and its heated swimming pool is open all year. Other resort facilities include tennis, fishing, horseback riding, skiing, snowmobiling, hiking, and skating. A recreation barn is popular with younger guests, and the nine-hole golf course, at 9,000 feet, is considered to be one of the most spectacular in the country. The Lodge's restaurant features seafood, steaks, and prime ribs of beef. Drinks are available in the Red Dog Saloon.

From The Lodge, one can see the entire Tularosa basin, with its Space Hall of Fame and great White Sands.

Accommodations: 50 rooms and suites, all with private bath. *Driving Instructions:* Take Route 82 from Alamogordo and go 19 miles east.

Las Cruces, New Mexico

INN OF THE ARTS

618 South Alameda Boulevard, Las Cruces, NM 88005. 505-526-3327. *Innkeepers:* Gerald and Linda Lundeen. Open all year.

Major Llewellyn came to New Mexico in 1881 as an agent for the Apache Indians, and his busy political life here included terms as district attorney and legislator for the territory. He also built two homes next door to each other before joining the Rough Riders.

Today the major's adobe houses have been joined by a modern addition that houses several common rooms, including a spacious living and dining room and a guest library. The traditional techniques of Mexican adobe construction are visible, including arched windows, mission tiles, kiva hearths, and patios. The fourteen guest rooms are each decorated around a particular American artist, with artwork provided by the Lundeen Art Gallery, next door to the inn. The Georgia O'Keefe Room has a queen-size bed and its own balcony; the Frederick Remington Room has a wet bar, kiva fireplace, and antique double bed; the Ray Swanson Room has a small kitchen, Taos bed, and balcony. Guests gather in the living room, with its eighteen-foot-high ceiling, for late afternoon drinks and hors d'oeuvres. In the morning, a Continental breakfast is served.

Accommodations: 14 rooms with private bath. *Pets:* Not permitted. *Children:* Under 12 not permitted. *Driving Instructions:* Take I-10 or I-25 to Las Cruces. South Alameda is 1 block west of Main Street.

Mesilla, New Mexico

MESON DE MESILLA

1803 Avenida de Mesilla, Mesilla, New Mexico. Mailing address: P.O. Box 1212, Mesilla, NM 88046. 505-525-9212. *Innkeepers:* Chuck and Merci Walker. Open all year.

Meson de Mesilla, behind old cottonwood trees with the Organ Mountains as a backdrop, was built to reflect the traditional Southwest Pueblo style of architecture, with its carved columns and beams, vigas, Mexican tile floors, and wooden ceilings. Chuck and Merci built the Meson in 1984, filling its rooms with antiques collected throughout the southwest. Rooms are cooled by ceiling fans as well as by central air-conditioning, while the decorative tilework and white walls are complemented by wood ceilings and antique furniture. Two large suites have working fireplaces, and all guest rooms have brass beds. The guest rooms open onto a second-floor balcony with a guest sitting area and also onto a second-story veranda that encircles the inn, where one can watch the lights of distant Las Cruces.

Full breakfasts are served to overnight guests in the dining room and atrium. Sunday brunch, midweek lunches, and candlelit dinners featuring Continental food are served to the public. The grounds include a swimming pool and putting green, and the Walkers provide bicycles for local touring.

Accommodations: 13 rooms and suites, all with private bath. *Pets:* Only small dogs permitted. *Children:* Under 12 not permitted. *Driving Instructions:* The inn is about 3/4 mile south of the Old Mesilla Highway 28 exit, off I-10.

It sometimes comes as a shock to Easterners, but Santa Fe was already established as a seat of government ten years before the Pilgrims set foot on Plymouth Rock. On Santa Fe's historic plaza stands the *Palace of Governors,* the oldest public building in America. The plaza was once the site of one of Billy the Kid's brief episodes as a captive and housed a bull ring in the mid-nineteenth century. Today, Pueblo Indians display their wares—pottery, jewelry, and homemade bread —daily. The Palace, built in 1610, was the seat of government for three hundred years. It is now a state museum.

THE BISHOP'S LODGE

Bishop's Lodge Road (Route 22), Santa Fe, New Mexico. Mailing address: P.O. Box 2367, Santa Fe, NM 87501. 505-983-6377. *Innkeeper:* James R. Thorpe, Jr. Open late March through October. Bishop's Lodge is a full-service resort in the foothills of New Mexico's Sangre de Cristo Mountains, about five minutes north of the Santa Fe Plaza. A century ago, Archbishop Lamy, immortalized in Willa Cather's book *Death Comes for the Archbishop,* wandered through the foothills of these mountains and found "Villa Pintoresca," a little ranch that had been planted with blooming fruit trees by the Franciscan Fathers in the early sixteenth century. The archbishop purchased the ranch for a retreat home, planted an orchard, and rebuilt the adobe house that stood on the hill overlooking the Rio Grande valley. To the house he added a private chapel that survives today. After the archbishop's death the retreat was purchased by publisher Joseph Pulitzer, who constructed two pretentious summer homes on the ranch for his daughters. In 1918, the entire property was sold to the late James Thorpe, a Denver mining man. The lodge has grown considerably in the more than sixty years the Thorpe family has owned and managed it. The architecture is largely Spanish Territorial in style, and the resort retains the flavor of old Spain.

The hacienda-style buildings are surrounded by informal gardens, and the balance of the 1,000 acres have been left in their natural state. The resort offers the elegance of grand hotel dining and accommodations but manages to capture a more intimate feeling by restricting its number of guest rooms. Many have exposed brick walls, Indian wo-

ven rugs, and exposed-beam ceilings. A number have fireplaces that guests may use.

The dinner menu at Bishop's Lodge changes daily, and might start with such offerings as chilled gazpacho, eggs à la Louis, smoked oysters, or cream of cauliflower soup. Among the daily entrées might be sautéed lamb chops, steak au poivre, fried oysters, or veal Oscar. The complete dinner includes vegetables, bread and rolls, dessert, and a beverage. The public is welcome to dine at Bishop's Lodge.

Resort activities include horseback riding, trap and skeet shooting, tennis (on five courts), swimming in a full-size pool, and use of the whirlpool bath and saunas. Children are offered a special summer-season program supervised by trained counselors.

Accommodations: 60 rooms and suites with private bath. *Pets:* Not permitted. *Driving Instructions:* The lodge is 3 miles north of the Santa Fe Plaza on Bishop's Lodge Road.

EL PARADERO

220 West Manhattan, Santa Fe, NM 87501. 505-988-1177. *Innkeepers:* Ouida MacGregor and Thom Allen. Open all year.

El Paradero is a family-owned and -operated inn on a quiet side street in Santa Fe, just two blocks west of the capitol building. It began as an adobe farmhouse in the early 1800s, with water brought in by one of the country's earliest irrigation ditches. A series of extensive remodelings in the 1880s and in 1912 added Victorian and Territorial touches to the rambling inn, but the present innkeepers have recaptured much of the early adobe look of clean, rounded lines and sparkling white walls.

The inn, with its enclosed courtyards, fireplaces, tiled floors, common rooms, and many nooks and crannies, is a friendly, casual place that appeals to artists, musicians, and families. A guitar and piano set out in the living room encourage an atmosphere of spontaneity in which impromptu concerts, slide shows, and lectures occur often. The innkeepers pride themselves on their unusual breakfast offerings, which include pear crepes with lemon-bourbon sauce, huevos rancheros, and, on occasion, a Kenyan dish of Maridadi eggs.

Accommodations: 12 rooms, 6 with private bath. *Driving Instructions:* From I-25, take the Old Pecos Trail exit and drive into town. Turn left on Paseo de Peralta, right on Galisteo, and left on Manhattan.

GRANT CORNER INN

122 Grant Avenue, Santa Fe, NM 87501. 505-983-6678. *Innkeepers:* Louise Stewart and Martin "Pat" Walter. Open all year except January.

Grant Corner Inn is a recently renovated manor house surrounded by a white-picket fence, flower gardens, and a gazebo. Within, every inch of the building has been pampered by Louise, a designer and graduate of the Cornell School of Hotel Management, and her husband, Pat. Tieback curtains at the windows, overstuffed chairs and sofas done in attractive fabrics, Oriental and American Indian rugs, paddle fans, wall coverings, and an array of antique beds are but a few of the touches that make Grant Corner an unusual place. Modern amenities in the guest rooms include both televisions and telephones. Baskets of fresh fruit are set out, and bathrooms have monogrammed towels and imported soaps. For guest rooms that share baths, terrycloth bathrobes are provided for the trips down the hall.

Grant Corner Inn was for years the home of Judge Robinson, who married scores of couples in the parlor. Today the room serves as a gathering spot where complimentary wine, red-pepper jelly, and cheese is served each evening.

It doesn't take long to realize that Louise is a fan of rabbits in every shape and form — from napkin rings and teapots to custom-made rabbit jewelry featured in the inn's country store. Breakfast, the only meal served except for holiday dinners, is a special event, with plum-cottage cheese pancakes, *heuvos rancheros,* stuffed French toast, or green chile crepes. In addition to the eleven guest rooms at the inn, there are also two rooms available in Louise and Pat's hacienda.

Accommodations: 13 rooms, 7 with private bath. *Pets and children under 5:* Not permitted. *Driving Instructions:* From Albuquerque, take I-25 to the St. Francis exit. Drive east to Alameda and turn right. Turn left on Guadalupe and then right on Johnson and proceed to the corner of Grant.

LA POSADA DE SANTA FE

330 East Palace Avenue, Santa Fe, NM 87501. 505-983-6351. *Innkeeper:* Dottie Reed. Open all year.

La Posada de Santa Fe sits on 6 shady landscaped acres in 375-year-old Santa Fe. At an altitude of 7,000 feet, the city is encircled by the dramatically beautiful Sangre de Cristo Mountains. *Posada* means resting place, and the heart of this inn is an authentically restored Victorian mansion built in the 1880s by Abraham Staab. The restaurant and bar overlook a patio and a fountain. The dining room, where all meals are served to guests and the public, is ornately decorated with many pieces dating back to the Spanish era. Guests are housed in adobes that display the Spanish influence with deep-welled windows, beehive fireplaces, carved Southwestern furniture, and gaily colored woven fabrics on whitewashed walls. Accommodations are available in a variety of sizes, including individual guest rooms, suites, and one- to three-bedroom casitas with separate living rooms and kitchenettes. Many rooms have hand-cut wooden ceilings with log rafters, known as vigas. La Posada is a short walk from the historic plaza of Old Santa Fe. There is an outdoor pool at the inn, and Taos Ski Valley and the Santa Fe Ski Basin are within an easy drive.

Accommodations: 100 rooms with private bath. *Pets:* Not permitted. *Driving Instructions:* From I-25 take the Old Pecos Trail turnoff to Pasco de Peralta. Drive two blocks to East Palace Avenue and turn right to the inn.

PRESTON HOUSE

106 Faithway Street, Santa Fe, NM 87501. 505-982-3465. *Inn-keeper:* Signe Bergman. Open all year.

Being one of only two Queen Anne–style Victorian buildings in New Mexico was sufficient reason to place this 1886 building in the National Register of Historic Places. It is likely one of very few Queen Annes built with a Spanish-style tin roof. Within, Preston House is also an eclectic blend of styles, probably reflecting a highly diverse group of construction workers: The stairway leading to the second floor, for example, has an Oriental look that may have resulted when coolies from an Episcopal work camp across the street were employed to build the stairs. A half-oval window lights the stairway landing, which is a popular spot for couples to gather and enjoy champagne in by the late afternoon sunlight. Downstairs, the parlor has a stained-glass window, maple-trimmed fireplace, and oak floor. A guest room on the first floor also has curved stained glass.

Originally built by a land speculator, George Cuyler Preston, who helped carve up the Southwest territories at the end of the Civil War, the house was later occupied by Dr. Louis E. Polhemus, an herbalist and dietician who had a faithful following among those who eschewed conventional medicine. Among the inn's many amenities are four working fireplaces. (A masseuse is available, with advance notice.) Guest rooms have pretty wallpapers, lace curtains, fluffy comforters on brass beds, and bowls of fresh fruit. Rocking chairs grace the front porch.

Accommodations: 6 rooms, 4 with private bath. *Pets and children under 12:* Not permitted. *Driving Instructions:* Take I-25 north from Albuquerque for about an hour. Exit at Old Pecos Trail, turn right to Paseo de Peralta, turn right at Palace and left onto Faithway Street.

RANCHO ENCANTADO

Highway 22, Tesuque, New Mexico. Mailing address: Route 4, Box 57-C, Santa Fe, NM 87501. 505-982-3537. *Innkeepers:* John T. and Betty Egan. Open from April to January.

Rancho Encantado is a sprawling Southwestern ranch-inn. The main lodge and outlying buildings appear to have been here since the first Conquistadores arrived. Not so: These low adobe and brick ranch-style houses were built recently, using styles and materials traditional to the Southwest. The main lodge was built in the early 1920s, the others quite a bit later. The energetic owner, Betty Egan, and her family have completely transformed this formerly modest guest ranch into a fine resort.

The buildings stand against the backdrop of the Sangre de Cristo Mountains, and the 168-acre ranch is encompassed almost entirely by the Santa Fe National Forest, rolling desert, and the Tesuque Indian Reservation. The big ranch lodge's guest rooms are up a natural tile-and-adobe staircase on the inn's top floor. The interiors of the

rooms and suites are quietly simple and look like old Western-movie sets, as well they should; much of the ranch has been used for just that purpose. The rooms have white adobe walls, wooden ceilings with exposed beams, and handmade tiles everywhere. There are smooth, rounded adobe fireplaces and Franklin stoves in the guests' quarters. The furnishings are antiques from all over the world, blending with Indian artifacts and woven rugs. The quarters range from intimate bedrooms to luxurious suites to complete housekeeping casitas. The Egans recently enlarged the ranch to include thirty-six condominiums in the nearby hills.

The dining room and bar, on the ground floor of the main lodge, offer dining on several levels. As with all the rooms, adobe walls, natural tiles, and wood-beamed high ceilings combine with the warm earth colors used throughout, both in the Egans' choice of fabrics and leathers and in the many Indian weavings, artifacts, and rugs. The restaurant serves thick, juicy steaks and ribs, the traditional spicy foods of the Southwest and Mexico, and Continental haute cuisine. Amazingly, the specialty at Rancho Encantado is fresh seafood; it is flown in from the coast every weekend, and there is a special seafood menu on Friday nights to celebrate the flight.

The ranch maintains a stable of horses and vast acreage in which to ride. In addition to the horses, the resort ranch offers swimming, tennis, and shuffleboard. If you see people who look familiar, they probably are; this unique resort has been host to hundreds of world-famous personalities. Many come back to vacation at this beautiful spot where they slaved under hot lights and greasepaint as old Western heroes or villains.

Accommodations: 22 rooms and suites with private bath; 36 condominiums. *Pets:* Not permitted. *Driving Instructions:* Rancho Encantado is on Route 22, 8 miles north of downtown Santa Fe.

Silver City, New Mexico

BEAR MOUNTAIN GUEST RANCH

Bear Mountain Road, Silver City, New Mexico. Mailing address: P.O. Box 1163, Silver City, NM 88062. 505-538-2538. *Innkeeper:* Myra B. McCormick. Open all year.

Bear Mountain, a bird or wildflower fancier's paradise, is a 160-acre ranch in a forest of pinon pine and juniper adjoining the Gila National Forest. Temperatures here, at an elevation of 6,250 feet on the Continental Divide, are relatively mild in all seasons, including summers. The main house was built in 1930 in the Spanish Territorial style with thick, white plastered walls and a red tile roof. The decor takes guests back to the feeling of the 1920s and 30s. In addition to the main house, there are three other smaller houses with bedrooms and kitchens on the property.

In the main house, guests gravitate to the sunny bird-watching room, where many of the meals are served while jackrabbits and quail entertain outside. The family-style meals here offer one entrée each day accompanied by plenty of fresh local vegetables and freshly baked muffins and biscuits. Nearby are trails through the Gila Wilderness and National Forest and the Gila River Bird Habitat.

Accommodations: 7 rooms and suites with private bath, plus three detached cottages. *Driving Instructions:* Take Route 180 to Silver City and turn north on Alabama Street. Drive 2.8 miles, crossing the first cattle guard. Turn left onto the dead-end dirt road and drive .6 miles to the main house.

Taos, New Mexico

Taos and surrounding towns are renowned for their beauty. Artists and writers flock to the peaceful 7,000-foot-high town in the towering, rugged mountains. To the west of Taos, Route 64 crosses the deep *Rio Grande Gorge* on a bridge 650 feet above the river. The river is wild and dangerous here. White-water fans ride the rapids through the remote wilderness.

THE TAOS INN

Paseo del Pueblo Norte, New Mexico. Mailing address: P.O. Drawner N, Taos, NM 87571. 505-758-2233; toll-free: 800-TAOS-INN from outside New Mexico. *Innkeeper:* Bruce Ross. Open all year.

The Taos Inn was built in the early nineteenth century as a private home, although some sections go back as far as the seventeenth century. The inn is constructed of adobe, with some walls almost 4 feet thick. In 1982, it underwent extensive restoration, earning it a niche in the National Register of Historic Places. The lobby has, as its centerpiece, a fountain on the site of the old town well. The original vigas (peeled logs) are still here, rising from the edge of the fountain to the rafters two stories above. Cocktails are served here and in the Adobe Bar, which has live entertainment by local musicians. Doc Martin's, the restaurant, serves original and traditional New Mexican specialities as well as fresh seafood and New American cuisine.

The guest rooms are decorated with locally crafted "Taos style" furniture, Southwestern antiques, and handwoven Indian bedspreads. Three-quarters of the rooms have pueblo-style fireplaces designed by Carmen Velarde, whose adobe work can be seen at the Smithsonian Institution in Washington, D.C. Mexican-style tiled bathrooms, cable color television, and private room telephones add to the comfort.

The inn is a center for the arts in Taos. Many artists' work is displayed here, and tours of the artists' studios and homes, as well as evening talks, can be arranged through the inn's management. The inn hosts two annual Meet-the-Artist series where guests have the opportunity to meet Taos artists, tour studios, attend lectures, and see on-the-spot demonstrations. (October 15–December 15 and May15–June 21.

Accommodations: 40 rooms with private bath. *Pets:* Not permitted. *Driving Instructions:* The inns is 1/2 block north of the plaza on Route 3 (Paseo del Pueblo Norte), the road to the Taos Pueblo.

Utah

ALTA LODGE

Alta, UT 84092. 801-742-3500. *Innkeeper:* Bino Levitt. Open mid-November to early May and mid-June to mid-October.

Alta, a mecca for powder skiing, is the home of Alta Lodge, one of the best-loved ski lodges in America. Set at 8,600 feet in Little Cottonwood Canyon, the buildings are surrounded by magnificent 11,000-foot peaks of the Rockies, with chair lifts just seconds from the door. The main building is of gabled wood with a copper roof. Built in 1940, the lodge has seen the recent completion of major steel-and-glass additions designed by architect John Sugden. The additions, which house saunas and two large whirlpool tubs, have panoramic views of High Rustlers Mountain. The dining room offers a variety of unusual dishes not generally found in the area, including grilled Pacific Coast abalone, bouillabaisse, and fresh escalope of salmon Troisgros. The kitchen at Alta Lodge is particularly proud of its rich chocolate soufflé, served with brandied whipped cream, a specialty that must be ordered at the start of a meal.

The many special features of Alta Lodge include the beauty and fresh air of its mountain location, the excellent skiing, and, in summer, the woodland trails, wildflower-covered hills, and crystal-clear mountain lakes and streams. Combine all these elements with an atmosphere of friendliness and caring in the tradition of the venerable European inns, and one can easily see why Alta Lodge has been attracting visitors from all over the world for almost half a century.

Accommodations: 56 rooms, 47 with private bath. *Pets:* Not permitted. *Driving Instructions:* From Salt Lake City take I-80 east to I-215. Follow I-215 south to Wasatch Boulevard. Take Wasatch Boulevard to Little Cottonwood Canyon, and drive up the canyon 9 miles to Alta.

Duck Creek and Cedar City, Utah

MEADEAU VIEW LODGE

Utah Highway 14 at Duck Creek Village, Utah. Mailing address: P.O. Box 356, Cedar City, UT 84720. 801-682-2495. *Innkeepers:* Harry and Gaby Moyer. Open all year.

Meadeau View is a small lodge constructed in 1964. A peeled-log exterior combines with low, wood-shingled roofs to blend harmoniously into the seemingly unending wilderness surrounding the lodge. Meadeau View is in a handsome setting 8,400 feet above sea level among aspens, pines, and wildflowers. The interior carries out the warm wood tones with carpeting and an abundance of pine paneling in all rooms. Guest rooms are on the lower level of the two-story lodge building, and suites are above. Regular rooms feature various combinations of queen, double, and twin beds. Some have French doors. The suites upstairs are large, with dormer windows that overlook the surrounding meadow. Each has a queen-size bed, pull-down divan, and complete modern bathroom. The lodge lobby has a geode-faced circular fireplace with swivel chairs around it.

The lodge is in the midst of the Dixie National Forest, about 45 miles from Zion and Bryce Canyon national parks. Most guests come for enjoyment of this scenic area. Meals are simple, family-style affairs featuring home-baked breads and rolls and a daily entrée.

The wilderness area around Duck Creek is fast becoming a popular cross-country ski area. To meet the needs of skiers, Meadeau View Lodge has put in a cross-country ski rental shop.

Accommodations: 6 rooms and 3 deluxe suites, with private bath. *Pets:* Not permitted. *Driving Instructions:* The lodge is 30 miles east of Cedar City on Route 14. It is 11 miles west of the intersection of Routes 14 and 89.

CENTER STREET BED & BREAKFAST INN

169 East Center Street, Logan, UT 84321. 801-752-3443. *Innkeepers:* Clyne and Ann Long. Open all year.

In 1877, several prominent members of the community invited Doctor Oliver Ormsby to serve as the area's first college-trained physician. His home, built two years later, is now the Center Street Bed & Breakfast Inn. The twenty-room brick Victorian, fronted by a brick-walled terrace, was remodeled in 1920 and still retains the wallpapers from that restoration. The Longs' collection of antiques is displayed throughout, with each guest room featuring something special. One has floor-length windows draped with ruffled lace, while another has a king-size, oak, four-poster bed and stained-glass windows in its bathroom. Breakfast is served by a staff member dressed in typical late-nineteenth-century costume. Not everything is from the Victorian era, however. The garden suite, for example, sports a canopied waterbed and a heart-shaped marble Jacuzzi, and the Longs provide videocassette recorders in the guest rooms. There is little doubt that Clyne and Ann had fun renovating the Victorian carriage house, behind the inn, which houses their "environmental suites"—one, the Desert Oasis, with a king-size round bed, a sultan's tent, and stars in the ceiling; another, Jungle Bungalow, filled with life-sized wild animals, trees, and exotic flowers, a waterfall, murals, and environmental sounds. There are more—be sure to ask.

Accommodations: 10 rooms, 4 with private bath. *Pets:* Not permitted. *Children:* Under 9 not permitted. *Driving Instructions:* Take Route 89 or Route 91 to the center of Logan. From Main Street, turn east on Center and drive 2 blocks.

MANTI HOUSE INN

401 North Main Street, Manti, UT 84642. 801-835-0161. *Innkeepers:* Jim and Sonya Burnidge and Alan and T.K. Plant. Open all year.

Manti House Inn's traditions go back to the the turn of the century, when it was owned by a prominent Utah churchman, John McAllister, who lived there with his nine wives. The stone inn, constructed of rare oolite limestone with eighteen-inch-thick walls that create deep window casings, was built in 1868 by one of the town's settlers, Richard Van Buren.

When the present innkeepers purchased the building, it had been abandoned for twenty years. Today, its guest rooms and suites have lacy white curtains, handmade quilts, antique bedsteads, and period lighting fixtures. The individual touches include an old straw bonnet ringed with dried flowers hanging on a bedpost and a little doll tucked into the lacy white pillows on an antique settee.

Wood-burning fireplaces and woodstoves are especially welcome after a nighttime horse-drawn buggy ride. There is a modern spa tucked into a plant-filled gazebo. Dinner, served to guests and the public in the dining room on tables with white embroidered linens, is a five-course event with a different single entrée each evening. Full breakfasts are served to guests only.

Accommodations: 6 rooms with private bath. *Pets:* Not permitted. *Smoking:* Not permitted. *Driving Instructions:* The inn is on Route 89.

Midway, Utah

THE HOMESTEAD

700 North Homestead Drive, Midway, Utah. Mailing address: Box 99, Midway, UT 84049. 801-654-1102. *Innkeeper:* Stan Heal. Open all year.

The Homestead, one of Utah's oldest resorts, was founded in 1886 by Swiss-born Simon Schneitter. Right in the middle of his farm was a "hot pot," or warm springs, that attracted neighbors who enjoyed bathing in the naturally warm mineral waters. Slowly the waters' fame spread, and soon the demand for warm-springs bathing overcame Schneitter's need to continue farming. Thus he opened his resort, "Schneitter's Hot Pots," and began to both feed and bathe his guests. Many of the original buildings are still in use, and there have been a number of additions since then. The result is an eclectic blend of architectural styles from rustic to Victorian to contemporary. Accommodations are in seven buildings. Many rooms are furnished with antiques; others have contemporary furnishings.

The Homestead, a full-service resort, has as its premise its strikingly natural setting on 60 acres of rolling countryside surrounded by mountains. Resort-style facilities include a heated swimming pool, hot tub, therapy pool, mineral pool, sauna, horseback riding, sleighrides in the winter and hayrides in the summer, lawn games, tennis, snowmobiling, boating, and cross-country skiing. In addition to the resort's activities, there is downhill skiing at Park City and Sundance.

Simon's is the Homestead's dining room, where guests may have breakfast, lunch, or dinner. Convention facilities are available also.

Accommodations: 43 rooms with private bath (in some cases, shower only). *Pets:* Not permitted. *Driving Instructions:* From Salt Lake City, take I-80 to Heber-Denver exit, Route 40. Follow Route 40 about 15 miles to the sign saying "Homestead." Turn right and follow the signs about 5 miles to the resort.

Park City, Utah

THE OLD MINERS' LODGE

615 Woodside Avenue, Park City, Utah. Mailing address: P.O. Box 2639, Park City, UT 84060. 801-645-8068. *Innkeepers:* Hugh Daniels, Susan Wynne, and Jeff Sadowsky. Open all year.

The Old Miner's Lodge, which overlooks well-known ski runs and the Wasatch Valley, was built in the late 1890s as a boardinghouse for silver miners—two of the old mines are just up the hill behind the lodge. The innkeepers have restored the lodge, infusing it with what might be called a Victorian atmosphere with a western flair and decorating each guest room in a way that captures the life and times of a local historical character. The Black Jack Murphy Room has a unique "mine shaft" entrance that opens into a small antique-filled room with views of the valley, while the Jedidiah Grant Room has an enclosed sun porch.

This is a casual place where guests make friends at afternoon wine-and-cider get-togethers or at breakfast, both served in the living room. Lunch and dinner are available for groups of six or more by advance arrangement.

Accommodations: 7 rooms, 4 with private bath. *Pets:* Not permitted. *Driving Instructions:* From I-80, take Route 224 south to Park City, where it becomes Park Avenue. From Park, turn right on Eighth, go 1 block to Woodside, and turn left.

WASHINGTON SCHOOL INN

543 Park Avenue, Park City, Utah. Mailing address: P.O. Box
536, Park City, UT 84060. 801-649-2341. *Innkeeper:* Sharon
MacQuoid. Open all year.

Park City is a blend of old and new, where turn-of-the-century miners'
houses dot steep hills alongside three major ski resorts. The newest
ski lift operates just 150 yards from the inn, once a schoolhouse. The
1889 stone building, rescued from disrepair and renovated in 1985,
is topped with a tower whose bell once called children to school. The
innkeeper welcomes guests to a Victorian inn complete with period
antiques that furnish the several public rooms, including a well-stocked
library and a living room where guests frequently gather by the fireside.
Breakfast is served in the dining room. There is an indoor spa with
steam bath, whirlpool, and sauna.

Accommodations: 15 rooms with private bath. *Pets:* Not permit-
ted. *Children:* Under 12 not permitted. *Driving Instructions:* From
Salt Lake City, take I-80 east to Route 224, which becomes Park
Avenue in Park City.

PULLMAN BED AND BREAKFAST INN

415 South University Avenue, Provo, UT 84601. 801-374-8141. *Innkeepers:* The Morganson family. Open all year.

Pullman Inn is an elaborate Victorian mansion built at the turn of the century as the private estate of Mayor William H. Ray. The Morganson family restored the hand-carved woodwork and furnished the rooms with family antiques and Victorian-style reproductions. There is a working fireplace in the parlor and several guest sitting areas on the upper landing. A circular staircase winds up to the landing and the guest rooms, where antique needlepoint decorates several walls. The second-floor rooms, with their Victorian furnishings, are more formal than those on the third floor, which have stenciled floors and colorful handmade quilts. Fresh bouquets of flowers and trays of the Morgansons' hand-dipped chocolates add to the inn's appeal. The chocolates and quilts, made by the Morgansons' mother, are also offered for sale in the gift shop. Full breakfasts are served family style in the dining room daily; dinner is served on Friday and Saturday evenings only.

Accommodations: 6 rooms, 4 with private bath. *Pets:* Not permitted. *Driving Instructions:* From I-15, take the University Avenue exit.

Saint George, Utah

SEVEN WIVES INN

217 North 100 West, Saint George, UT 84770. 801-628-3737. *Innkeepers:* Donna and Jay Curtis and Allison and Jon Boweutt. Open all year.

Seven Wives Inn was built in the heyday of Utah's pioneers and its outlawed polygamists. The builder, one Mr. Woolley, while not a polygamist himself, sympathized with them and cleverly incorporated secret escape routes and a hidden room into the adobe-walled home he built in 1873. Donna and Jay Curtis, along with daughter Allison and her husband, Jon, discovered these in the process of tucking bathrooms into alcoves of the spacious guest rooms.

Each guest room bears the name of one of Donna Curtis's grandfather's wives. "Sarah" is a suite of rooms complete with sun parlor. Here, the primitive pine furniture includes an old church pew in front of the fireplace. A teddy bear sits patiently on the pew, waiting to be cuddled. "Melissa," named for wife number one, is the most luxurious room, with its set of American oaken pieces that include a towering bedstead and an oak-rimmed tin bathtub.

The Curtises have done a fine job restoring this pioneer homestead, preserving the 18-inch-thick adobe walls and original painted pine moldings. They make their own soaps and often provide dishes of homemade candy or bowls of fresh fruit in the guest rooms. Room television sets, a swimming pool, and a hot tub are provided.

Accommodations: 9 rooms with private bath. *Driving Instructions:* Take I-15 to the Saint George exit. Follow signs to Brigham Young Winter Home. The inn is diagonally across the street.

Salt Lake City, Utah

BRIGHAM STREET INN

1135 East South Temple Street, Salt Lake City, UT 84102. 801-364-4461. *Innkeepers:* John and Nancy Pace. Open all year.

Walter Lyne's parents, Thomas and Carrie Cogswell Lyne, were unique people. In Salt Lake City Thomas coached drama, wrote poetry, and even delved into spiritualism. He and his wife became active mediums and conducted many séances. About 1870 the Lynes made a sudden and curious departure from Utah, abandoning their son Walter. The reason for their departure is still unknown. Walter, who eventually became a successful wool broker and remained one for the rest of his business career, built the mansion that became the Brigham Street Inn.

The house had two and a half stories when it was originally built, largely of brick and red sandstone mined from Emigration Canyon. Golden oak and bird's-eye maple were used for trim inside the mansion. Touches of Queen Anne and Classical Revival are evident in the architecture of the house. Much of the exterior is intact and features an asymmetrical yet formal facade, eight upstairs dormer windows, and a separate carriage house.

The interior of the inn was designed by its owner architect John Pace and finished by a team of twelve Salt Lake City designers and craftsmen. Each designer was assigned to work on a room, either one

of the guest rooms or the parlor, living, or dining room. Although each of the rooms is unlike the others — an "Oriental" room with a balcony is next to an "Art Nouveau" room furnished with antiques, while upstairs a room designed in dark blue is reminiscent of a man's study — the overall effect is of a relaxed elegance that strikes one as a cohesive whole.

The parlor and the living and dining rooms are all "common areas," open to all guests and *their* guests to meet, drink coffee or tea, read the newspapers provided by the inn, exchange ideas, and so forth. A Steinway grand piano is available to those who wish to play. Original artwork hangs in every room and hallway. A complimentary Continental breakfast is served every morning in the dining room, which contains a hand-embroidered seventeenth-century tapestry worked by Tibetan nuns and an eighteenth-century Chinese scroll.

Five guest rooms contain working fireplaces, and all of the common rooms have the original nineteenth-century fireplaces, with wooden mantels and imported tiling. Every guest room has a telephone, color television, and a clock radio. The Garden Suite, a favorite of honeymooners, has a private entrance, apartment-sized modern kitchen, mirrored bedroom, and double Jacuzzi bath.

Accommodations: 9 rooms with private bath. *Pets:* Not permitted. *Driving Instructions:* The inn is about a mile east of Salt Lake City's center, at the corner of South Temple and R streets.

ELLER BED AND BREAKFAST

164 South 900 East, Salt Lake City, UT 84102. 801-533-8184. *Innkeepers:* Lavon and Margaret Eller. Open all year.

The Eller Bed and Breakfast was built at the turn of the century and is listed in the National Register of Historic Places. The house appears to be unscathed by time: Its original oak woodwork and stained or leaded glass is in remarkably fine condition. The sliding oak doors separating the front and back parlors are intact, and the kitchen still sports its Great Majestic coal and wood stove.

The Ellers have furnished the inn with period oak and walnut pieces softened by colorful samplers and stitchery. Guests enjoy getting together in the old-fashioned parlor with its piano, while a sitting room housing the television is also a social place in the evenings. The Ellers are experts on Salt Lake City and the surrounding canyons and ski areas—they even provide a sauna for weary skiers and claim that it is likely to put enough zip back in them for a night on the town. Temple Square, ten blocks west of the inn, is a leading tourist attraction in Salt Lake City. The Great Salt Lake itself is about ten miles away and, in addition to boating, provides the novelty of swimming in a ''sea'' in which it is almost impossible to sink. The Ellers provide a Continental breakfast of fruit, coffee and tea, juice, and hot muffins or breads.

Accommodations: 5 rooms with shared baths. *Smoking:* Not permitted. *Pets:* Not permitted. *Driving Instructions:* From Temple Square, drive 10 blocks east on South Temple Street to the 900 East block; turn right and go 1 1/2 blocks.

Wyoming

Alta, Wyoming

INN LOST HORIZON

Targhee Ski Resort Road, Alta, Wyoming. Mailing address: RD 1, Box 3590, Driggs, ID 83422. 307-353-8226. *Innkeepers:* Chuck and Shigeko Irwin. Open all year.

Named in honor of James Hilton's novel, this modern restaurant and inn is in a scenic corner of northwest Wyoming, overlooking the eastern slopes of the Grand Tetons. Chuck Irwin designed the inn as his home, and it houses his extensive collection of international primitive art, gathered during a twenty-year tour of duty with the Air Force. The retired colonel and his wife first created an Oriental restaurant at Lost Horizon, spending the better part of the day preparing the elaborate ten-course Japanese and Chinese dinners. Guests don hand-knit slippers to enjoy hors d'oeuvres and wine by the fireside, and should plan to spend three or four hours enjoying their meal.

Following the success of their restaurant, the Irwins opened several guest rooms. The enthusiastic response has inspired the Irwins to expand both dining and guest rooms, and a large hexagonal addition is near completion. For overnight guests, many recreational opportunities are nearby, including the Snake River and Grand Teton and Yellowstone national parks, both within an hour's drive.

Accommodations: 4 rooms, 2 with private bath. *Pets and children:* Not permitted. *Driving Instructions:* From Jackson, take Route 22 and (Idaho) Route 33 to Driggs, Idaho. The inn is 6 miles east of Driggs, near the Idaho border, on the Targhee Ski Resort Road.

Atlantic City, Wyoming

"MINER'S DELIGHT" INN AND RESTAURANT

Atlantic City, Wyoming. Mailing address: Box 205, Lander, WY 82520. 307-332-3513. *Innkeepers:* Georgina and Paul Newman. Open May through New Year's Eve.

The "Miner's Delight" is really out of the way. The chinked log structures of the old hotel are at 7,660 feet in the Wind River Mountains of the Shoshone National Forest. Today, Atlantic City, an old gold mining town, boasts a population somewhere between ten and fifty, with an unknown number of ghosts. The "Miner's Delight" Restaurant's fame is countrywide. It is a nationally known gourmet restaurant with reviews in major American food magazines and newspapers. Ensconced in the 1895 log cabins that housed the old Carpenter's Hotel are the innkeepers, Paul and Gina Newman. It may be a great surprise to many to find such a fine restaurant in a tiny mountain ghost town, and it is an even bigger surprise to meet the cosmopolitan Newmans, an attractive, sociable New York couple. In the early 1960s, Paul had taken a year off from his high-powered Madison Avenue ad firm to reduce his high blood pressure, when he announced to Gina that they weren't going back to New York: "I'm not going to die on Madison Avenue." When Gina recovered from the shock, she agreed, on the condition that they buy the old Carpenter Hotel. So it was that the two Newmans left their prestigious jobs, Gina as a magazine editor and Paul as an adman. They both enrolled in a variety of cooking schools, including James Beard's and Dione Lucas's, and even a sauce course at the Sorbonne. Amid dire predictions of "impossible," the place opened. The predictions of failure were based on solid reasoning: There was (and still is) no menu, the rates were fairly high, the food was to be international cuisine in a land of "I'll eat anything as long as it's steak," and the nearest customer was 35 miles away. The place was a fantastic success. Reservations must be made several weeks in advance for the very popular five-course dinner.

Although "Miner's Delight" is primarily a restaurant, it does maintain three small guest rooms in the hotel and three small, primitive chinked-log cabins for dinner guests who wish to spend the night. The hotel rooms have twin beds.

Each room in the inn has its own individual flair. Decorations are paintings, Paul's area photographs, antiques, and examples of old advertising art. Handwoven Navaho rugs are scattered on polished wood floors. The dining room, heated by an old army stove from Fort Stambaugh, has a wall of floor-to-ceiling windows and gray wood walls brightened by canary yellow bentwood chairs and flower-bedecked tables. The Saloon is a spacious room with pots of geraniums in front of the picture windows.

In the old days in Atlantic City, a "miner's delight" was a flash of gold in the pan; today, it has to mean the international cuisine of the Newmans' kitchen. Diners are treated to a full five-course dinner served from 6 P.M. to midnight. For a prix fixe, diners receive, by candlelight, a steady stream of dishes, beginning with appetizers that might include shrimp La Fonda, a fondue, coquilles Saint-Jacques, or the specialty of the house, a pâté maison. Soup could be a Senegalese curried chicken, a fresh broccoli, or black bean; the main courses run from an Italian manicotti with homemade noodles to a French coq au vin, Hawaiian pork, shrimp Creole, or a boned chicken Florentine. Fresh vegetables, salads, breads, and desserts complete the meal. This is indeed a special place.

Accommodations: 3 rooms, 2 with private bath; 3 cabins without indoor plumbing. *Pets:* Not permitted. *Children:* Under 12 not permitted. *Driving Instructions:* From Landers take Route 28 for about 29 miles to a left turn onto a dirt road marked Atlantic City. It is 3 miles over this well-graveled road to "Miner's Delight".

BIG HORN MOUNTAIN BED AND BREAKFAST

Route 335, Big Horn. Mailing address: P.O. Box 579, WY 82833. 307-674-8150. *Innkeepers:* Bobbie and Ron Spahn. Open all year.

Big Horn is in the piney mountains of northeastern Wyoming, bordering Big Horn Mountain forestland and offering hundred-mile views from the porches. The innkeepers—Ron is a geologist and former Yellowstone Ranger and Bobbie is a nurse—and their two children, Heather and Eric, built this solar-powered log home and the nearby cabin themselves. The inn is a peeled-log building with a big deck and a three-story log and pine-paneled living room furnished with dark wicker and soft-cushioned upholstered couches. There are fireplaces and an outside deck. The main house has two guest bedrooms, and the secluded cabin offers kitchen facilities, a porch, and a bedroom as well as a sleeping loft. The Spahns provide a Continental breakfast and help guests plan the day's activities. The inn is 15 miles from Sheriden and I-90, but there are deer, turkey, and moose on the grounds and even an occasional bear or passing mountain lion. There are hiking trails and good fishing nearby.

Accommodations: 2 rooms with private bath; 1 cabin with bedroom, sleeping loft, and kitchen. *Smoking:* Not permitted. *Driving Instructions:* From Exit 25 off I-90, drive south on Route 87 to Route 335. Continue south to the inn on the left.

Cody, Wyoming

IRMA HOTEL

1192 Sheridan Avenue, Cody, WY 82414. 307-587-4221. *Innkeeper:*
Stan Wolz. Open all year.

Many people have built hotels. Bill Cody built a hotel too. He also
built the town where it stands. In 1894, Cody heard tales of the Big
Horn Basin just over the mountain from Sheridan, Wyoming, where
he owned a lavish hotel. In the next few years he and several influen-
tial investors formed the basis of a company set up to develop and
promote the area. Promotion was Cody's long suit. He had an almost
magical sense of good theater. His Wild West Show was the smash
hit of North America and Europe. At a performance in England, he
had driven a stagecoach with the Prince of Wales riding shotgun and
four crowned heads of European countries inside. It was therefore
an easy matter for Cody to enlist financial supprt for his "Shoshone
Land Development" project. By 1897 the rudiments of a town had
been established and named "Cody" in his honor. In 1902 Buffalo
Bill began construction of the Irma Hotel, named in honor of his only surviving daughter.

Cody was not a man to withhold money from any deserving project, and the Irma was no exception. In the end the project cost $80,000,
a princely sum in 1902. Portions of the exterior walls of the Irma were
constructed from locally gathered river stones, but most of the building

was done with cut sandstone quarried nearby. In the years that followed, the Irma grew as did the town, with large additions in 1929 and a smaller addition in 1978.

Guests at the Irma may choose from rooms that retain the old-fashioned splendor of the Cody era and more modern rooms in the 1929 and 1978 additions. The fifteen "original" suites offered in the older section are formed from what were originally thirty guest rooms. The suites now each contain private bathrooms. During the restoration process, wallpapers similar to the original Victorian papers were chosen for each suite, and many of the original dressers, rockers, tables, and bedsteads were retained. New springs and mattresses were installed in each bed. Drapes were added to the rooms in place of the original pull shades, and carpeting was installed to cover the hardwood floors. Many of the bathrooms have retained claw-foot tubs and ornate marble wall sinks. Probably the most popular of these rooms is the Buffalo Bill Suite, where guests may sleep on the showman's original bed and enjoy the furnishings of the two-room suite he designed especially for himself. Each of the other fourteen suites in the old section of the Irma is named for a famous Wyoming hero.

On the Irma's first floor is its famous grill room. The dining room contains what is generally considered the most elaborate back bar in the West. The large cherrywood bar runs the length of the room and bears unusually fine carving and other ornamentation. The back bar was a gift to Cody from Queen Victoria in appreciation for his command performance in 1900. It was made in France, shipped to New York by steamer, then by rail to Red Lodge, Montana, and finally by horse-drawn freight wagon to Cody. In the early days of the Irma, the present dining room was the bar and billiards room. It now contains many early photographs showing cowboys standing at the bar while others shoot pool in the background.

The Irma serves a traditional selection of Western food at all three meals. The dinner menu features roast prime ribs of beef as a house specialty as well as five or six cuts of steak and four daily "steam table" specials. Typical of the latter are barbecued spare ribs and braised sirloin tips with noodles made in the Irma kitchen.

Accommodations: 41 rooms with private bath. *Driving Instructions:* Cody is at the intersection of Routes 14, 16, 20, 14A, and 120 in northwestern Wyoming. The Irma is in the center of town.

Evanston, Wyoming

PINE GABLES BED AND BREAKFAST INN

1049 Center Street, Evanston, WY 82930. 307-789-2069. *Innkeepers:* Arthur and Jessie Monroe. Open all year.

The Pine Gables Bed and Breakfast Inn is a Victorian mansion built in the Eastlake style in 1883 by a successful local banker and sawmill owner. The mansion, with its six redwood gables, once stood alone on a hillside on the outskirts of town. Evanston grew since then, and the inn now stands at the edge of its business district. The innkeepers will take interested guests on an evening walking tour of historic Evanston.

A 50-foot hallway with Victorian parlors on either side dominates the ground floor. The inn is furnished throughout with Victorian antiques, and there is an antique and collectables shop. Each guest room is decorated with a unique collection of Victorian pieces. The Oak Room has two 6-foot-tall carved oaken beds, as well as a Murphy bed; and another room contains Eastlake furnishings and a fireplace. The Anniversary Suite has two antique-filled rooms, as well as an old-fashioned bathroom with claw-footed tub and pedestal sink.

The innkeepers know the area well, and they will supply guests with a map and a picnic lunch. The nearby Uinta Mountains have more than five hundred lakes and are a photographer's, hiker's, and birder's paradise. There are many historic sites in the area, as well as plenty of outdoor recreation.

Accommodations: 6 rooms, 4 with private bath. *Pets:* Small pets permitted. *Driving Instructions:* Evanston is at the junction of I-80 and Routes 89 and 150 and U.S. 189, in the southwestern corner of Wyoming.

Glenrock, Wyoming

HOTEL HIGGINS

416 West Birch, Box 741, Glenrock, WY 82637. 307-436-9212. *Innkeepers:* Jack and Margaret Doll. Open all year.

The Hotel Higgins was built in 1916 by a coal-mine developer, John Higgins. The modest exterior gives few clues to the workmanship inside, where there is darkly stained mahogany and cherry woodwork, and many of the floors are hexagonal terrazzo in earth tones and red. Ornate lighting fixtures, beveled glass, and delicately etched windows are found throughout the hotel.

Margaret and Jack Doll bought the property in 1974 and restored it to its early elegant appearance and atmosphere. One of their first tasks was to restore and reopen the hotel's dining room. They hired a chef who had trained at the Culinary Institute of America. The restaurant, named the Paisley Shawl for an heirloom of Margaret Doll's, was an instant success. People often drive for hours for one of its meals. There is a bar, lounge, and extensive wine cellar.

Once the restaurant was a success, the Dolls turned their attention to restoring the guest rooms on the two upper floors, furnishing them with some of the hotel's original pieces, including brass and iron antique bedsteads and walnut dressers as well as heirlooms from the Dolls' collections. All these efforts have earned the inn a place in the National Register of Historic Places. A full, "elegant" breakfast is served to guests, either in their rooms or on the porch.

Accommodations: 11 rooms, 8 with private bath. *Pets:* Not permitted. *Driving Instructions:* The hotel is just off I-25 at the Glenrock exit, on the main street.

JENNY LAKE LODGE

Jenny Lake Loop Road, Grand Teton National Park, Wyoming. Mailing address: P.O. Box 240, Moran, WY 83013. 307-733-4647.

Innkeeper: Clay James. Open early June through mid-September.

Jenny Lake Lodge grew up gradually from a homestead started in 1922 by Tony Grace. Won over by the beauty of the area, he began that year to build the log structures that remain today as part of the Jenny Lake Lodge complex. He planned a dude-ranch operation and built a main lodge and five guest cabins. He named his new business "Danny Ranch" after the daughter of a close friend who was one of his first guests. The original cabins continue to provide overnight accommodations, and the first lodge is the lounge in the present-day main building. In 1931, Grace sold his holdings to the Snake River Land Company, which had been sponsored by John D. Rockefeller, Jr., as part of his plan to include the valley floor in Grand Teton National Park. Three years later, the ranch management was taken over by the Grand Teton Lodge Company, and the property was expanded by the addition of more cabins. In the mid-1950s the lodge complex was enlarged once again with a new kitchen for the main building and private bathrooms for each cabin.

The main building and the thirty cabins are built of logs. The lounge is constructed of logs for the walls and ceilings and native stone for the fireplace. The floors are all of hardwood, with throw rugs. Within each guest room are two easy chairs, a writing desk, a chest of drawers, and beds with headboards adapted from the original bedsteads. The rustic but comfortable accommodations harmonize with the natural setting. Each cabin bears the name of a local flower. Jenny Lake Lodge has five two-room fireplace suites that may be rented by couples but are a better buy for groups of three or four. There is no television and no bar. Although the lodge is rustic, there is an undercurrent of elegance, especially in the dining room, where perhaps more than elsewhere at Jenny Lake the Rockefeller touch of Rockresort management can best be felt. Because Jenny Lake operates on the modified American plan, guests have full choice of the breakfast and dinner menus. With advance reservations, the public is welcome at all three meals.

Breakfast consists of a choice of eggs, done any style, bacon,

sausage, blueberry pancakes, Belgian waffles, and French toast. Picnic lunches are always available, as well as a dining-room luncheon menu. Every evening there is a different dinner menu resplendent with items from appetizers to desserts. Typical starters include a ramekin de fromage made with a Swiss cheese produced locally, king crab and salsify cocktail, and hot shrimp Oregon à l'Absinthe. Two freshly made soups are offered daily, followed by the choice of five entrées. Recent offerings included fillet of sole meunière with almonds, broiled mushrooms; duckling à l'orange; filet mignon béarnaise; veal picatta; roast chicken forestière; and poached Columbia River salmon. A choice of two salads follows the entrée, and then come dessert and a beverage. Every Sunday the lodge has a very popular buffet dinner for which reservations are a must.

Jenny Lake Lodge is a short walk from the lake, and horseback riding is available on the property. The setting and small size of this rustic resort combine to produce a tranquillity not found in the more populated parts of Grand Teton National Park. All income from the lodge and the Grand Teton Lodge Company in general is used not only for their own operation but also to further the conservation activities of Jackson Hole Preserve, Inc., a nonprofit educational conservation organization.

Accommodations: 30 cabins with private bath. *Driving Instructions:* The Lodge is 20 miles north of Jackson on Teton Park Inner Road.

Medicine Bow, Wyoming

VIRGINIAN HOTEL

P.O. Box 127, Medicine Bow, WY 82329. 307-379-2377. *Innkeepers:* Vickie and Vern Scott. Open all year.

For years, one of our closest friends used to tell us story after story of her early childhood spent in Medicine Bow, playing in the streets of the sleepy town and sliding down two stories of banisters at the Virginian Hotel, one of the few buildings in town of such height. We were thrilled to discover that the old Virginian Hotel is gradually being returned to its early Western style.

August Grimm set out to construct his "modern" hotel in 1909, seven years after Owen Wister had published the novel for which Grimm's hotel was named. The building was constructed of concrete blocks that were poured into molds on the construction site, a common practice at the turn of the century. The entire structure was completed in the fall of 1911. The white oak trim and stairwell were brought to the town in rough form by railroad and finished at the site. The leaded ceilings were manufactured in Saint Louis and also delivered by rail. The bar in the saloon was handmade from a load of pine and poplar off the back of a truck. Outside, a board sidewalk and a hitching post survive from an earlier era.

In the 1940s, in conformity with fashion, ceilings were lowered, walls paneled, doors added, and fixtures changed. The Virginian did not escape such modernization. However, in the past five years, efforts have been made to return the Virginian to its original decor. Old pictures and descriptions in the local newspapers and from older community citizens have guided the restoration. The tile ceilings are being removed, and the leaded ceilings refurbished. Hardboard floors and wainscoting are being replaced. Renovation continues; the Owen Wister Dining Room has been completed and furnished with antiques. The second and third floors are finished, with the installation of period wallpapers, brass or iron beds, and early furnishings. Twelve of the rooms on the second and third floors consist of antique furnishings, each different from the other. An imposing brass four-poster more than a hundred years old graces the Wister Suite. Highboard walnut is found in another, oak in a third, and carved walnut in yet another. Two rooms have cavalry bunks from the Medicine Bow supply depot of the 1870s, and all the rooms contain commodes, hardwood dressers, or old antique wardrobes. The feeling of the rooms captures the Westward movement. Throughout are the memories of gamblers, gunfighters, cattle barons, and homesteaders. In addition to the hotel rooms, there are nineteen in an adjacent motel.

Food is served at the Virginian in the Eating House (open 6 A.M. to 10 P.M.) and in the dining room. The Eating House offers a wide selection of sandwiches and grill items as well as several complete dinners. The dining room, named in honor of Owen Wister, offers a special of the day as well as steaks, chops, and seafood.

Accommodations: 20 hotel rooms, including 4 suites, with shared baths; 11 motel rooms with private bath. *Pets:* Not permitted in the hotel rooms. *Driving Instructions:* Take I-30-287 north from Laramie or Walcott to Medicine Bow, or take Route 287 south from Casper to Route 487, which leads directly to Medicine Bow.

MEDICINE BOW LODGE AND GUEST RANCH

Route 130, Saratoga, Wyoming. Mailing address: P.O. Box 752, Saratoga, WY 82331. 303-326-5439. *Innkeepers:* Mary Behan and David Cheney. Open all year.

Medicine Bow Lodge stands on 75 acres in the Medicine Bow National Forest at an altitude of 8,000 feet. The lodge is in a remote area, 20 miles southeast of Saratoga. The Sierra Madre and Medicine Bow mountain ranges provide a panoramic backdrop for the high-plains Platte Valley. Roaming herds of deer, elk, and antelope are familiar sights at the lodge, as are bear, beaver, fox, and coyote in the surrounding hills. Two mountain trout streams cross the property and offer excellent fishing. The main lodge and eight cabins are mountain-style log structures built in the early 1920s. The chinked-log cabins, each with a private bath and propane heat, sleep up to six people.

The rustic lodge is a favorite with guests. A spacious living room and nearby game room are good places to get to know fellow lodgers or just relax. The dining room serves three family-style meals a day. The public is welcome; many travelers just enjoy stopping by for coffee and a wedge of freshly baked pie. Guests are entertained by the brightly colored hummingbirds that come and go at the dining-room window's feeders. Horseback riding is the featured attraction here, and the horses are surefooted creatures well used to the mountain and forest trails.

In winter the cross-country skiing and snowmobiling at the ranch are excellent. Winters there are quite exciting, as the temperature occasionally drops well below zero. The cabins at such times have no plumbing, and guests must use the bath facilities in the spa and sauna lodge nearby. It is a time for enjoying a songfest around the fire and swapping tales of adventures experienced along the trails of Medicine Bow National Forest.

Accommodations: 8 cabins with private bath. *Driving Instructions:* From Saratoga take Routes 130 and 230 south for 8 miles. Turn east on Route 130 when it leaves Route 230. Go 12 miles to the lodge entrance on the south side of the highway. There are signs to the lodge at the entrance.

GOFF CREEK LODGE

Routes 14, 16, and 20, Shoshone National Forest, Wyoming. Mailing address: P.O. Box 155, Cody, WY 82414. 307-587-3753. *Innkeeper:* Gloria Schmitt. Open mid-May to mid-October.

Goff Creek Lodge is in the beautiful Wapiti Valley, just 10 miles from the east entrance of Yellowstone National Park. Goff Creek was first occupied in 1905 by John Goff, who used it as his hunting camp. The renowned hunting guide and buffalo hunter acted as the personal guide to President Theodore Roosevelt on his American big-game hunts and was highly spoken of in Roosevelt's memoirs as both a personal friend and an outstanding guide.

Goff Creek Lodge consists of a main lodge and a group of log cabins in the pine and fir timber of the Absaroka Rockies, between two mountain ridges bounding Goff Creek. The creek, a white-water, spring-fed mountain stream, flows past the cabins on its way to the Shoshone River below. The lodge was built in 1910 and was completely renovated in the 1960s. The main lodge has a warm, Western feeling created by its peeled-log walls, exposed-log and plank ceilings and ranch-style oaken furniture. Guests gather here for dinner, which is served at tables under the wagon-wheel-and-hurricane-lamp chandelier. On cool days a fire burns in the stone fireplace in the center of one wall. The dinner menu offers turkey, chicken, ham steak, fried shrimp, and boneless mountain trout, a lodge specialty. Accompanying the meal are home-baked breads and, for dessert, pies and cheesecake. Lucky fishermen may have their catch of the local cutthroat trout prepared for either breakfast or dinner. The lodge is a convenient base for exploring Yellowstone National Park, and the cook will gladly pack a box lunch to be enjoyed at a park picnic area later in the day. The lounge carries on the Western motif, with lamps made from boots, authentic Navaho rugs, and hunting trophies and Indian artifacts on display.

The cabins, most containing two guest rooms, are of the peeled-log construction mandated in the national forest. Each has pine-paneled walls decorated with horse and other Western pictures, exposed-beam and plank ceilings, and Western-style furnishings.

Accommodations: 14 rooms with private bath. *Driving Instructions:* The lodge is 41 miles west of Cody on Routes 14, 16, and 20.

ELEPHANT HEAD LODGE

Wapiti, WY 82450. 307-587-3980. *Innkeepers:* Joan and Phil Lamb and daughters Gretchen and Nicole. Open all year.

The Elephant Head Lodge, named for its proximity to a local rock formation, is a half-moon arrangement of ten cottages around a very early log cabin lodge and dining room. The lodge and the "honeymoon" cabin were both built in 1910 by Buffalo Bill's niece and her husband. The lodge has been maintained with its original peeled-log interior and exterior, with a large stone fireplace at one end and a bar at the other. Flanked by rock cliffs on two sides and surrounded by pine trees, the lodge is but a few feet from the trout-filled Shoshone River.

Each of the ten cabins exhibits the log exterior mandated by the national forest. The cabins have wall-to-wall carpeting, antiques, and peeled-log furniture, an unusual type of furniture handmade from 5-inch-diameter pine logs assembled into beds and tables without the use of nails. Needless to say, the beds are massive. The cabins all have individually controlled heat and private bathrooms, and the honeymoon cabin has its own working fireplace. There is also a fireplace in the main lodge, with a fire going in the early morning and the evening every day.

The log dining room, next to the main lodge, serves three meals daily, of which both breakfast and dinner are served to the public as well as guests.

Activities at the Elephant Head Lodge include wilderness trail rides on horseback, fishing in the Shoshone River, and backpacking or exploring in Yellowstone Park, 11 miles from the lodge. Indian artifacts are still found in the area. Local game includes moose, elk, deer, and bear. Movies are shown nightly in the main lodge. The Lambs provide airport pickup and car rentals for guests on the American plan.

Accommodations: 10 cabins with private bath. *Driving Instructions:* The lodge is on Routes 14, 16, and 20 about 40 miles west of Cody and 11 miles east of the east entrance of Yellowstone Park.

Yellowstone National Park, Wyoming

OLD FAITHFUL INN

Yellowstone National Park, WY 82190. 307-344-7311. *Innkeeper:* The Yellowstone Park Division of TW Services. Open early May to mid-October.

The Old Faithful Inn is actually the second one built near the famous geyser. The original burned in 1894 and was not immediately replaced because a regulation prohibited building within ¼ mile of any park attraction. The original had been illegally placed closer, and backers of the hotel felt that to build farther away would detract from the hotel's popularity. Finally the ruling was changed and plans were laid to construct the present hotel ⅛ mile from Old Faithful.

In 1902 a young architect, Robert C. Reamer, was selected to design the new hotel. Construction began in 1903 and continued through the long, bitter winter until completion in 1904, just before the park opened that year. The primary building materials were native to the area. All the logs and the twisted supports so clearly seen in the lobby and throughout the old portions were gathered nearby. The stone, including the 500 tons required for the huge fireplace, was quarried on the road to West Thumb. The original building contained 140 rooms and was described as the largest log hotel in existence.

Entrance doors to the inn are made of massive split logs and have hand-wrought hardware. The central lobby, the showplace of the hotel, is 64 feet square and rises 85 feet to the ridgepole. Dormer windows, later to become one of Reamer's trademarks, light the ceiling. Four overhanging balconies descend the walls and offer views of the large rough-stone fireplace and its big clock embedded in the stone. The clock keeps accurate time even today, after seventy years. The clock, the copper light fixtures, and all other hardware in the building were designed by Reamer and wrought by a blacksmith on the site.

Over the years, the pressures of overflow crowds visiting the park required two wings to be added to the original building. Both the 1913 and the 1928 wing were designed by Reamer to harmonize with his original plan.

There are three types of rooms at Old Faithful Inn. The newest are in the 1928 wing and have been thoroughly modernized. The "private bath" rooms are a compromise between fully modernized and rustic. Some have their peeled-log walls exposed but have fully modern baths. The rooms in the original hotel are the most historic and reminiscent of a visit to Yellowstone at the turn of the century. These have

split-log doors, exposed peeled-log interiors, and, in many cases, the original iron or brass beds. The rooms, lighted by early wall sconces, have all been carpeted. Many overlook the geyser, and some have bay windows with sitting areas. These rooms are in great demand, but if guests request them well in advance, the staff will try to accommodate the requests. In any event, there is a second-floor outdoor balcony that has a fine view of the geyser.

The dining rooms in each of the Yellowstone Park hotels and lodges have a menu that is redesigned for each season. For this reason it is impossible to predict exactly what food services will be available in any specific place. In general, however, each has a full menu at all three meals.

Accommodations: 364 rooms, 196 with private bath. *Driving Instructions:* The inn is only a couple of hundred yards from the Old Faithful geyser, just off the southwestern Grand Loop road that circles the interior of the park. Access to the road is through any of the five main gates.

Index of Inns

WITH ROOM-RATE AND CREDIT-CARD INFORMATION

Inns are listed in the chart that follows. In general, rates given are for two persons unless otherwise stated. Single travelers should inquire about special rates. The following abbreviations are used throughout the chart:

dbl. =   double. These rates are for two persons in a room.

dbl. oc. = double occupancy. These rates depend on two persons being registered for the room. Rentals of the room by a single guest will usually involve a different rate basis.

EP =   European Plan: no meals.

MAP =   Modified American Plan: rates include dinner and breakfast. Readers should confirm if stated rates are per person or per couple.

AP =   American Plan: rates include all meals. Readers should confirm if stated rates are per person or per couple.

BB =   Bed and Breakfast: rates include full or Continental breakfast.

Credit-Card Abbreviations

AE =   American Express   MC =   MasterCard
CB =   Carte Blanche   V =   Visa
DC =   Diners Club

Important: All rates are the most recent available but are subject to change. Check with the inn before making reservations.

Send us your name and address... ...and we'll send you a free gift.

If you purchased this book, we'd like your name and address for our mailing list. Just supply the information below, and we'll send you your free gift.

I purchased this book at:

☐ Atticus
☐ Barnes & Noble
☐ B. Dalton Booksellers
☐ Bookland
☐ Books Inc.
☐ Crown Books
☐ Encore Books
☐ Hunter's Books
☐ J.K. Gill

☐ Kroch's & Brentano's
☐ Lauriats
☐ Marshall Field & Co.
☐ Paperback Booksmith
☐ Readmore
☐ Stacy's
☐ Taylors
☐ Upstart Crow & Co.
☐ Waldenbooks

Other:_____   (City)_____

I purchased this book on (approximate date):_____

Please send my free gift to:

Name:_____

Street or Box:_____

City_____State_____Zip_____

Please mail to:
The Compleat Traveler, c/o Burt Franklin & Co., Inc.
235 East 44th St., New York, N.Y. 10017 U.S.A.

Limit: One per customer.   **Limited time offer.**   M

THE COMPLEAT TRAVELER'S READER REPORT

To: *The Compleat Traveler*
    c/o Burt Franklin & Co., Inc.
    235 East 44th Street
    New York, New York 10017 U.S.A.

Dear Compleat Traveler:

I have used your book in ＿＿＿＿＿＿＿＿＿＿＿＿＿ (country or region).
I would like to offer the following ☐ new recommendation, ☐ comment,
☐ suggestion, ☐ criticism, ☐ or complaint about:

Name of Country Inn or Hotel:

＿＿＿＿＿＿＿＿＿＿＿＿＿＿＿＿＿＿＿＿＿＿＿＿＿＿＿＿＿＿＿＿＿

Address: ＿＿＿＿＿＿＿＿＿＿＿＿＿＿＿＿＿＿＿＿＿＿＿＿＿＿＿＿＿

＿＿＿＿＿＿＿＿＿＿＿＿＿＿＿＿＿＿＿＿＿＿＿＿＿＿＿＿＿＿＿＿＿

Comments:

Day of my visit: ＿＿＿＿＿＿＿＿＿ Length of stay: ＿＿＿＿＿＿＿＿＿

From (name): ＿＿＿＿＿＿＿＿＿＿＿＿＿＿＿＿＿＿＿＿＿＿＿＿＿＿＿

Address ＿＿＿＿＿＿＿＿＿＿＿＿＿＿＿＿＿＿＿＿＿＿＿＿＿＿＿＿＿

＿＿＿＿＿＿＿＿＿＿＿＿＿＿＿＿＿＿＿＿ Telephone: ＿＿＿＿＿＿＿＿